Saint-Lô 1944

COMBAT

Fallschirmjäger

VERSUS

US Soldier

Frank Baldwin

Illustrated by Steve Noon

OSPREY PUBLISHING

Bloomsbury Publishing Plc

Kemp House, Chawley Park, Cumnor Hill, Oxford OX2 9PH, UK

Bloomsbury Publishing Ireland Limited,

29 Earlsfort Terrace, Dublin 2, Ireland

1385 Broadway, 5th Floor, New York, NY 10018, USA

E-mail: info@ospreypublishing.com

www.ospreypublishing.com

OSPREY is a trademark of Osprey Publishing Ltd

First published in Great Britain in 2025

A catalog record for this book is available from the British Library.

ISBN: PB 9781472867124; eBook 9781472867094;
ePDF 9781472867100; XML 9781472867117

25 26 27 28 29   10 9 8 7 6 5 4 3 2 1

Maps by bounford.com
Index by Rob Munro
Typeset by PDQ Digital Media Solutions, Bungay, UK
Printed by Repro India Ltd.

Osprey Publishing supports the Woodland Trust, the UK's leading
woodland conservation charity.

To find out more about our authors and books visit
www.ospreypublishing.com. Here you will find extracts, author
interviews, details of forthcoming events and the option to sign up for
our newsletter.

For product safety related questions contact
productsafety@bloomsbury.com

Artist's note

Readers may care to note that the original paintings from which the
color plates in this book were prepared are available for private sale. All
reproduction copyright whatsoever is retained by the publishers. All
inquiries should be addressed to:

https://www.steve-noon.co.uk/

The publishers regret that they can enter into no correspondence upon
this matter.

CONTENTS

Introduction

What could be more dangerous or frightening than landing on the beaches of Normandy, France, on D-Day, June 6, 1944, facing an enemy secure in concrete bunkers amid the bullets and shell splinters raining down on the infantrymen stranded on the open beaches? For the US Army's infantrymen, D-Day was just the beginning, the very start of a bitter battle among the *bocage* (hedgerow country) that lasted over six weeks. This would be a stiff test for US troops, demanding new tactics and a determination to beat some of Nazi Germany's most brutally effective troops. For *Fallschirmjäger* (parachute troops), recruited and trained to execute airborne assault landings, the Normandy battle would pitch them into combat against superior numbers backed by overwhelming firepower. Could confidence in their commanders and faith in the Führer prevail over the industrial war machine of the US Army? This is the story of the combat between US infantry and German *Fallschirmjäger* during the struggle in the hedgerow country of the Manche Department in western Normandy.

After the capture of Carentan and the establishment of a link between Utah Beach and the Cotentin Peninsula and Omaha Beach east of the Vire Estuary, the priority for the First US Army was to isolate and then capture the port of Cherbourg. German resistance in Cherbourg ended on July 1, 1944. The First US Army's next task was to push south to capture the city of Saint-Lô and secure an area from where US Army formations could stage a breakout. This was part of the plan outlined in the pre-invasion briefings in April and May 1944. The Allied commanders had anticipated that the Germans would make their main effort in the Caen sector – good open tank country – but this left the First US Army with the task of gaining enough ground and eroding sufficient German strength to launch a breakout. It had been hoped, in the D-Day plans, that by D+9 (June 16), Saint-Lô might be captured, but German resistance and the difficulties imposed by the hedgerow country resulted in delay.

This photograph taken in Carentan, June 1944, shows US troops of the 327th Glider Infantry Regiment (101st Airborne Division) pausing to examine a bullet-riddled sign pointing the way, south, to Paris and Saint-Lô and north to Cherbourg. Carentan was captured from German forces including Fallschirmjäger-Regiment 6 on June 13. This image illustrates the strategic situation facing the US Army. Its highest priority was to capture the port of Cherbourg, which was the task of the VII Corps, while the V, VIII, and XIX corps were to advance to Saint-Lô, before breaking out toward Paris. (Keystone/Getty Images)

The Allied planners knew of the hedgerow country. The western half of the Operation *Overlord* lodgment area was much closer terrain than that to the east, which was open country dotted with villages and woods. Thus, the bulk of Allied armor landed on D-Day was in the British Second Army sector. This was also where the Allies expected the Germans to deploy their armor, which meant the First US Army deployed fewer tanks in an area considered infantry country. This was not disclosed to the US troops before D-Day, however, so as to keep the site of the landings secret, which meant the hedgerow country surprised most US troops who fought there unless they happened to have trained in an area of Britain with similar small fields.

Published in June 1944, this propaganda image shows two *Fallschirmjäger* scanning the skies for Allied aircraft. The nearer man has his Kar 98k rifle to hand. (dpa picture alliance/Alamy Stock Photo)

The map shows the area between Carentan and Saint-Lô that was fought over in June and July 1944. The ground is cut with tributaries of the Vire River, and much of the area between Carentan and Saint-Lô is low-lying marshland. Higher ground has been intensively farmed to the east and west of the marshland for over 1,000 years. It is an area of small, irregular fields, often bounded by high and thick hedges. Over centuries, many hedgerows have grown over thick earth banks reinforced by the roots of shrubs and trees. The terrain nullified maneuver by vehicles and limited sight and engagement ranges, turning every field into a little fort.

Accordingly, the First US Army had four army corps (V, XIX, VII, and VIII) from east to west. Two army corps of the German 7. Armee opposed them. The LXXXIV. Armeekorps was originally responsible for defending what would become the D-Day invasion sector. In July, it had under command the remnants of the formations that escaped from the Cotentin Peninsula and reinforcing infantry formations from Brittany. In early July, it defended the 7. Armee's western sector. To the east, covering the sector from Saint-Lô to Caumont, was the II. Fallschirmkorps. This headquarters was established to command parachute divisions that were formed in France in 1943–44. Hermann Göring raised German airborne formations from surplus Luftwaffe personnel and volunteers. This unpromising material was commanded by cadres of veterans from the German airborne arm. Having stunned the world with their dramatic actions in Rotterdam, Narvik, Corinth, Crete and their stubborn defense at Monte Cassino, many German unit commanders were high-profile figures whose exploits were familiar from newsreels and newspapers.

The campaign in western Normandy would not be decided by armored maneuver but through hard fighting conducted by small groups of infantry in combat as intensive as any fought in either world war. It is easy to picture battles as arrows on battle maps in headquarters or history books, but such characterizations are often far removed from the desperate struggles between handfuls of men for patches of ground the size of a football field.

In this book, the focus is upon three engagements between the US Army's 2d, 29th, and 90th Infantry divisions and elements of the 2., 3., and 5. Fallschirmjäger-Divisionen, in an effort to cast light on their combat experience. Telling the story of how the fighting in western Normandy unfolded after D-Day, it examines the two sides' doctrine, weapons, morale, and will to win.

US troops and vehicles in Saint-Lô sometime after its liberation. The city was almost totally destroyed by 2,000 Allied bombers when they attacked German troops stationed there during Operation *Overlord* in June. (Galerie Bilderwelt/ Getty Images)

The Opposing Sides

ORGANIZATION AND STRUCTURE

Fallschirmjäger

Fallschirmjäger were volunteer members of the Luftwaffe rather than the Heer (German Army). The *Fallschirmjäger* arm was massively expanded in 1943 from one to seven *Fallschirmjäger-Divisionen* and a total strength of 160,000 men under the command of the newly designated 1. Fallschirmarmee. Göring's 1. Fallschirmarmee also established two corps headquarters. The I. Fallschirmkorps was in Italy, while the II. Fallschirmkorps was formed in France under the command of General der Fallschirmtruppe Eugen Meindl, an airborne veteran awarded the *Ritterkreuz* (Knight's Cross) for his gallantry in Crete, where, despite wounds received in landing, he was primarily responsible for capturing Maleme Airfield. He had subsequently commanded formations of Luftwaffe ground troops on the Eastern Front. His headquarters was formed in January 1944 in Melun, France, from that of the XIII. Fliegerkorps, which was redundant after the Luftwaffe field divisions were transferred to the Heer in late 1943. On May 12, the II. Fallschirmkorps took command of the 3. and 5. Fallschirmjäger-Divisionen, forming in Brittany. The 1. and 4. Fallschirmjäger-Divisionen served in Italy as part of the I. Fallschirmkorps.

While German corps did not usually have any units permanently assigned under their command, the *Fallschirmkorps* were an exception and notionally had several formations, all with the numerical designation 12: these included a reconnaissance battalion and a *Sturmgeschütz* (assault artillery) brigade as well as an artillery regiment and an antiaircraft artillery regiment, each with three *Abteilungen* (battalions). In reality, the corps artillery regiment was still forming in the summer of 1944 and did not take part in the Saint-Lô fighting.

Initially, *Fallschirmjäger* recruits had to meet specific physical criteria, including not suffering from motion sickness; they underwent rigorous training, including six parachute jumps. By 1944, however, only a minority of recruits had been jump-trained. Some 100,000 men were recruited into the airborne arm, but only 30,000 men were ever jump-trained; of these, 8,000 were trained before 1941. Most recruits seem to have joined as teenagers who volunteered for this arm. At the heart of each of the *Fallschirmjäger* formations were cadres of veterans, the leaders and trainers of the recruits.

The three *Fallschirmjäger-Divisionen* that fought for Saint-Lô were different. The 2. Fallschirmjäger-Division had been engaged in bitter fighting on the Eastern Front from late 1943 until May 1944 when the remnants were transferred to Brest in Brittany. In advance, the division's Fallschirmjäger-Regiment 6 had started to re-form in December 1943. Its commander, Major Friedrich August Freiherr von der Heydte, had been a senior staff officer in the 2. Fallschirmjäger-Division in Italy, and the cadre of NCOs were from six regiments and Fallschirmjäger-Brigade Ramcke, which served in North Africa. Fallschirmjäger-Regiment 6 had the luxury of conducting its own jump training for its teenage recruits in Wahn, Germany, using the barracks roofs in place of jump towers. According to Oberjäger Eugen Griesser, much of the time spent training involved close-combat exercises, made more realistic because the NCOs involved had substantial experience of battle conditions (Griesser 2011: 70). Oberjäger Dietrich Scharrer recalled that while Fallschirmjäger-Regiment 6 had previously been manned by jump-trained volunteers from the airborne arm, older soldiers like himself were now mixed with recruits straight from basic training and personnel from across the breadth of the Luftwaffe's operations; while he initially thought this was a bad idea, he found that the mixture was beneficial as the regiment focused on intensive *Gruppe*-level training (Griesser 2011: 70–71).

Major von der Heydte obtained some aircraft for jump training, and most of his regiment was parachute-trained. On May 2, Fallschirmjäger-Regiment 6 deployed to the Elsenborn military training area on the German–Belgian border and was inspected by Oberst Hermann-Bernhard Ramcke, the commander of the 2. Fallschirmjäger-Division, who later recalled the excellent state of training of the regiment and declared it ready for battle (Griesser 2011). The rest of the 2. Fallschirmjäger-Division was still on the Eastern

A *Fallschirmjäger* shouldering an MG 34 machine gun during the Low Countries campaign, May 1940. The MG 34 was the principal weapon of the German infantry *Gruppe* until 1942, when it began to be joined by the MG 42. (Scherl/Süddeutsche Zeitung Photo/Alamy Stock Photo)

A *Fallschirmjäger* MG 34 team in Tunisia, January 1943. This shows the positions in action of the three-man crew in a trench with a grenade for close-in defense. Note the lighter tropical uniforms not worn in Normandy. (ullstein bild/ullstein bild via Getty Images)

Front, however, and would not start moving back to Wahn to be rebuilt until May 20. It was still in Wahn on D-Day. Fallschirmjäger-Regiment 6 was sent to Normandy as an independent regiment and deployed as a reserve unit for LXXXIV. Armeekorps between Carentan and Mont Castré.

Fallschirmjäger-Regiment 6 was particularly strong. Heydte had acquired enough light machine guns to issue each *Gruppe* (section) with two rather than one MG 34 or MG 42. Most of the *Fallschirmjäger* were armed with the Kar 98k, while *Gruppe* leaders and their deputies were issued the MP 40. The regiment also had some FG 42s, while marksmen were equipped with the Gew 43. On May 18, Fallschirmjäger-Regiment 6 had three parachute battalions, each of three companies armed with 18 machine guns and three 8cm mortars. Each battalion had a heavy-weapons company with 12 machine guns, four 8cm mortars, and two howitzers. The regiment had three support companies, numbered 13 (nine 12cm mortars), 14 (four 7.5cm antitank guns), and 15 (*Pioniere*, with two 8cm mortars and six machine guns). In Normandy the regiment added a 16th (reconnaissance) company, plus antiaircraft, motor transport, supply and maintenance, and field-replacement subunits. Fallschirmjäger-Regiment 6's total strength was about 4,500 men.

Formed in October 1943 in the Reims area, the 3. Fallschirmjäger-Division moved to Brest on February 1, 1944. The division's three *Fallschirmjäger-Regimenter* were numbered 5, 8, and 9, and its support units bore the number 3. Each regiment consisted of three parachute battalions, each of three parachute companies and a heavy-weapons company, numbered from 1 to 12. In addition, according to a return dated May 22, 1944, each regiment had a 13th (heavy-weapons) company with heavy mortars or recoilless rifles and medium machine guns, a 14th company with two 7.5cm antitank guns (14./FJR 5 and 14./FJR 9) or nine 4.2cm antitank guns (14./FJR 8), and a 15th (pioneer) company with 3–7 machine guns and 4–9 flamethrowers.

The divisional artillery regiment had only one of its three battalions, I./Fallschirmartillerie-Regiment 3, equipped with four 10.5cm light howitzers and three 10.5cm recoilless guns in each of its three batteries.

Fallschirmjäger prepare to fire a 10cm Nebelwerfer 35 heavy mortar, Italy, 1943. The *Fallschirmjäger* arm took part in heavy fighting in Italy in 1943, gaining a reputation for determination, aggression, and endurance in actions such as Ortona, Monte Cassino, and Anzio. Veterans from these actions would be the cadres and leaders of the units that fought in Normandy. (michael cremin/Alamy Stock Photo)

Kurt Student reviews *Fallschirmjäger* of II. Fallschirmkorps. Promoted *Generaloberst* on July 13, 1944, Student was the pioneer of German airborne forces and since 1941 the commanding general of German parachute troops. In the war's closing months he led the 1. Fallschirmarmee, notably during Operation *Market Garden* in September 1944. (ullstein bild/ullstein bild via Getty Images)

The other two battalions were still forming in Germany. The division's Fallschirm-Pionier-Bataillon 3 had 33 machine guns and 22 flamethrowers. Fallschirm-Panzerjäger-Abteilung 3 was organized into three companies, each with three 7.5cm PaK 40 and four 4.2cm antitank guns. The division was established for an antiaircraft-artillery battalion, but it does not seem to have been issued any guns. Instead, the division had the 2. Fallschirmjäger-Division's antiaircraft-artillery battalion under command.

Generalleutnant Richard Schimpf, the 3. Fallschirmjäger-Division's commander, did not have a background in the airborne arm. A decorated World War I infantry veteran, he learned to fly and joined the new Luftwaffe, specializing in aerial reconnaissance. In 1942, he was assigned to command divisions of Luftwaffe ground troops until these were transferred to the Heer. Photographs show a rather portly figure compared to the lean veterans among his subordinates. The division's manpower on May 22 was 17,420, almost full strength, but there were still shortages of key equipment, according to Schimpf: "Machine guns, mortars and antitank weapons were lacking, and in transportation, we were still 50 to 60 per cent short of vehicles. The state of training and the striking power of the troops was good. Their fighting spirit could even be called very good. Eighty-seven per cent of the division had also completed the parachute training course" (War Dept 1946a: 1).

The division was described as "motorized," probably meaning that there was no provision for horses or horse-drawn transport. There was a wide variety of vehicle types and a shortage of spare parts. The division had enough ammunition for 3–6 days of combat. Compared to the rest of the German formations in France, the 3. Fallschirmjäger-Division was impressive. Well-trained, up to strength, and well-equipped, it was one of the few German infantry formations capable of offensive operations, with twice the strength of a 1944 infantry division.

The second division in the II. Fallschirmkorps was the 5. Fallschirmjäger-Division, formed in Brittany in March 1944 with cadres from the 3. Fallschirmjäger-Division. The divisional commander was Generalleutnant Gustav Wilke, a World War I veteran who served in the Reichswehr (the name given to Germany's armed forces during 1919–35) before transferring

About to arm his stick grenade, this *Fallschirmjäger* has been assigned as a grenadier for a German counterattack and carries his rifle slung over his shoulder. A volunteer in his early twenties, he admires his NCOs and officers, most of whom are veterans of many campaigns. He has a strong faith in the ethos of the *Fallschirmjäger* and the Führer, but he will be lucky to survive to become a prisoner.

Weapons, dress, and equipment

This young volunteer is armed with a Kar 98k rifle (**1**), stick grenades carried in grenade bags (**2**) under his arms, and "egg" grenades (**3**), carried on his belt. He wears an M38 helmet (**4**) with a canvas cover and an elasticated band for foliage, a *Splittermuster* camouflage smock (**5**), standard *Fallschirmjäger* trousers (**6**), and black boots (**7**). His Luftwaffe-pattern personal equipment includes rifleman's ammunition pouches (**8**), a bread bag (**9**), canteen (**10**), and bayonet scabbard (**11**).

General der Fallschirmtruppe Eugen Meindl with Generalfeldmarschall Erwin Rommel. Meindl was the commander of the II. Fallschirmkorps, raising it and commanding it in Normandy. He wears the *Edelweiss* badge on his field cap, a memento of his service in the mountain troops. Something of a legend within his arm, he made his first parachute jump into Narvik in 1940 and was seriously wounded on Crete in 1941. In August 1944 he was awarded the *Eichenlaub* (Oak leaves) to the *Ritterkreuz* in recognition of his troops' stubborn defense of Saint-Lô. (Picture Post/Hulton Archive/Getty Images)

to the Luftwaffe in 1935. He joined the airborne forces and was awarded the *Ritterkreuz* for his role in the Netherlands fighting in May 1940. He, too, had commanded a Luftwaffe field division before their transfer to the Heer and led the 2. Fallschirmjäger-Division on the Eastern Front during the winter of 1943/44. He assumed command of the 5. Fallschirmjäger-Division on April 1, 1944, rather late to ensure the division was best prepared for the forthcoming fight.

On May 22, the 5. Fallschirmjäger-Division had an authorized strength of 17,455, but only 12,253 were in post. The division had only 60 percent of its authorized manpower, 25 percent of its light weapons, 23 percent of its heavy weapons, and 9 percent of its vehicles. Fallschirm-Pionier-Bataillon 5 was supposed to have 738 rifles, but only had 38. The divisional antitank battalion should have had 36 7.5cm PaK 40, but only had three. Fallschirmjäger-Regiment 14 was established for 2,961 rifles, but only had 1,162. Heydte, the commander of Fallschirmjäger-Regiment 6, was harshly critical: "Less than 10% of the men had jump training, and at most 20% of the officers had infantry training and combat experience. Armament and equipment were incomplete, only 50% of authorised weapons; one regiment was without helmets, no heavy antitank weapons and not motorised" (Historical Division 1954).

The regimental commanders included veterans such as *Ritterkreuz* holder Major Wolf-Werner Graf von der Schulenburg, a veteran of Crete and Monte Cassino, who commanded Fallschirmjäger-Regiment 13. Major Herbert Noster, the commander of Fallschirmjäger-Regiment 14, had been wounded and captured in 1940 in the Netherlands, then released by the British after three years in captivity on account of the severity of his wounds. Fallschirmjäger-Regiment 15 was commanded by Major Kurt Gröschke, who had been decorated for preventing a breakthrough at Monte Cassino in January 1944.

The soldiers of the 5. Fallschirmjäger-Division have been described as a mixed bunch, with some fervent believers in the Nazi regime and others weary Eastern Front veterans who did not wish to fight (McKee 1984: 22–23).

US Army

The US Army's infantry division of 1944 was based on the triangular division of the 1930s. The combat element was provided by three infantry regiments, each divided into three battalions, with companies lettered from A to M (omitting J) within each regiment. Each battalion had a heavy-weapons company, and each regiment had a cannon company and an antitank company.

The United States passed a Selective Service Act in 1941, expanding the peacetime strength of the US Army. The men serving in the infantry were those left after the US Army Air Corps, technical services, and armor had selected the men they wanted, or in the case of airborne forces, those men who chose to volunteer to serve in that arm.

The original plan was to raise a 200-division army. Instead, fewer divisions were raised with a very large number of independent battalions of supporting troops such as armor, artillery, engineers, and independent infantry battalions. The division only included those elements that would always be needed. Tank, tank-destroyer, and antiaircraft battalions might be attached, as might additional artillery and engineers, meaning a US Army infantry division might, in practice, have far more units than the divisional table of organization and equipment might suggest.

Heavily laden troops of the 90th Infantry Division, their rifles encased in waterproof plastic, make their way aboard LCI(L)-326 toward Utah Beach. Elements of the 90th Infantry Division landed on D-Day. (Galerie Bilderwelt/ Getty Images)

This young soldier has been disturbed by a German attack. He is a replacement for one of the many hundreds of US soldiers lost in the early weeks of the Normandy fighting. Arriving at the front line with several dozen fellow replacements, he did not receive a unit induction before being assigned to a rifle company and taken forward to join his squad.

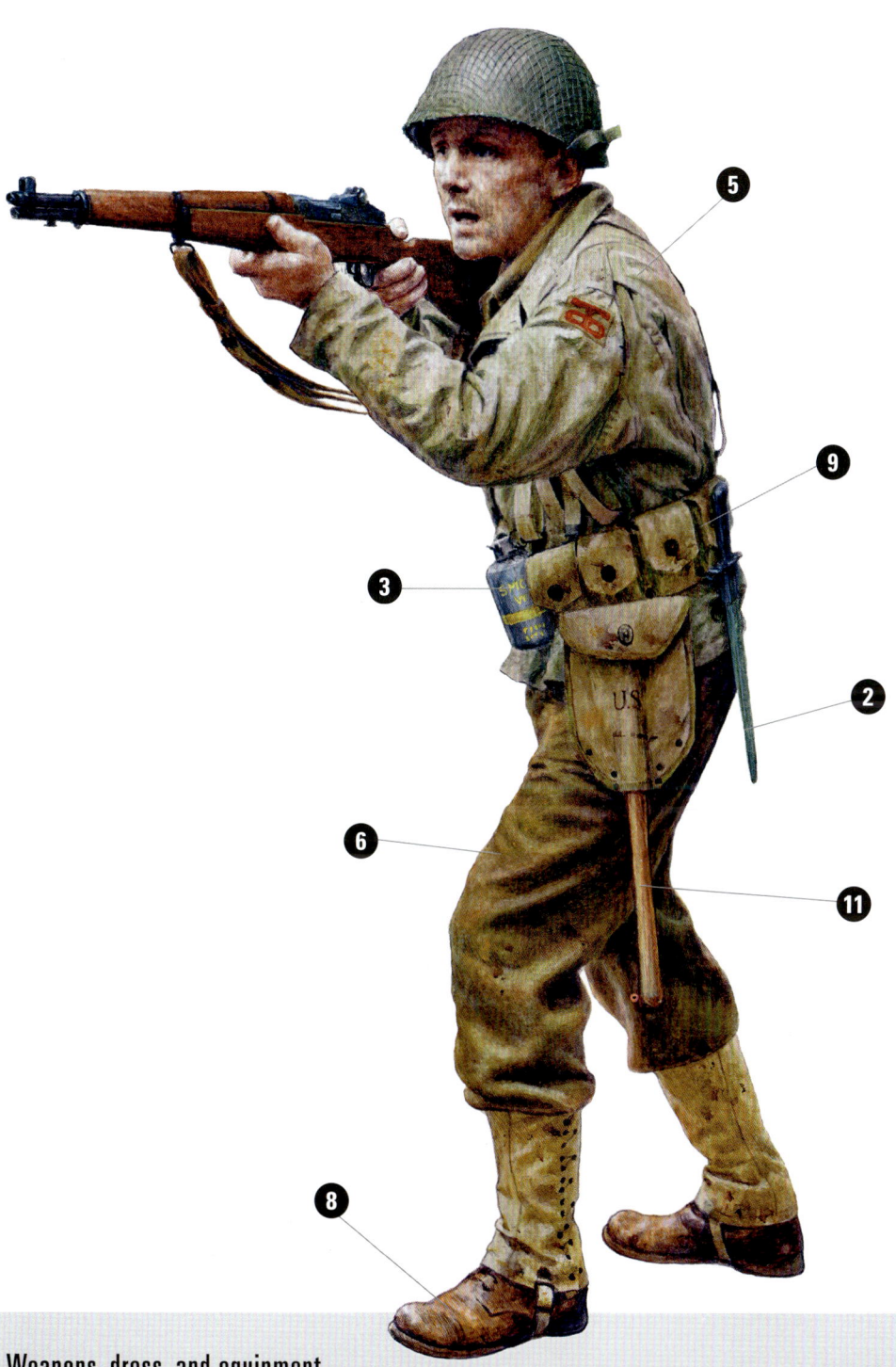

Weapons, dress, and equipment

He is armed with an M1 Garand rifle (**1**) and M1 bayonet (**2**) and carries an M15 WP (white phosphorus) smoke grenade (**3**) on his belt. He wears the standard steel helmet (**4**) with mesh net for foliage, the M1941 field jacket (**5**), wool trousers (**6**), leggings (**7**), and shoes (**8**).

He is wearing modified M1910 equipment (**9**) with a first-aid pouch (**10**), an entrenching tool (**11**) on his left hip, and a canteen (**12**) on his right hip. He also has a bandoleer (**13**) carrying rifle-ammunition clips slung over his shoulder.

By 1944, many of the soldiers in the infantry divisions that landed in Normandy had been in the US Army for years. The 2d Infantry Division was a regular formation, but its regular officers and NCOs had been repeatedly picked over to form the cadres for new divisions, which left its composition little different to that of more recently raised formations. The 29th Infantry Division was a National Guard formation, raised by the states of Maryland and Virginia, and some of the prewar guardsmen served in the Normandy fighting. One of its regiments, the 116th Infantry, was the Virginia Militia, which had served in the Confederate Army with distinction as the Stonewall Brigade. The 175th Infantry was recruited from the Baltimore National Guard, and the 115th Infantry was from rural Maryland. The division had deployed to Britain in 1942. Its first commander, Major General Leonard T. Gerow, was promoted to command V Corps in July 1943 and replaced by Major General Charles H. Gerhardt, who commanded the division during pre-invasion training and the subsequent fighting in Normandy. The 116th Infantry was part of the assault force that landed on Omaha Beach and suffered heavy casualties. The 90th Infantry Division was raised in 1942 from a cadre from the 6th Infantry Division.

US Army officers and NCOs were essentially wartime promotions. Junior officers were the product of wartime officer training programs – the famous "90-day wonders." Very few company, battalion, or regimental commanders – or their staff – had any prior combat experience except in formations such as the 1st and 9th Infantry divisions, which had served in the Mediterranean theater. The US Army had a higher proportion of officers than the German armed forces. The 29th Infantry Division, for example, was established for 800 officers for 15,000 men, while a *Fallschirmjäger-Division* had only about 300 officers for 17,000 men.

WEAPONS

Fallschirmjäger

The standard German individual weapon was the 7.92mm Kar 98k bolt-action rifle, adopted in 1935 and which remained in use throughout the war. The *Fallschirmjäger* in Normandy also used the 7.92mm Gew 43, a semiautomatic rifle 2cm shorter than the Kar 98k; the Gew 43 was issued in small numbers, about half with telescopic sights. Specifically designed for use by airborne troops, the 7.92mm FG 42 (*Fallschirmjäger-Gewehr*) select-fire automatic rifle was shorter but heavier than the Kar 98k and fed by a ten- or 20-round side-mounted magazine. With only 7,000 being manufactured, the FG 42 tended to find its way into the hands of officers and NCOs, normally armed with the 9mm MP 40, an effective close-range submachine gun out to 100yd.

The Germans saw grenades as a key infantry weapon, both in close battle against infantry and also in six-grenade *Geballte Ladungen* ("concentrated loads") against tanks. The Stielhandgranate 24 was a development of the World War I stick grenade (nicknamed "potato masher" by the British), with a shorter head and slightly longer "stick" (handle). As the name suggests, the smaller and lighter Eihandgranate 39 had an "egg-shaped" sheet-metal body. Smaller numbers of smoke grenades were also provided. Rifle grenades could be fired from the Kar 98k.

The main squad weapon of the *Fallschirmjäger* was the 7.92mm MG 34 or MG 42 light machine gun, the latter offering a higher rate of fire that was greatly appreciated in short, intense engagements. Both types were general-purpose machine guns: when fired from a bipod, they were squad light machine guns, but when mounted on a tripod, they functioned as medium or heavy machine guns, firing farther and in the indirect-fire role. In Normandy, *Fallschirmjäger* also made use of captured Allied automatic weapons when available, at least until the ammunition ran out. Judging by photographs, .30- and .50-caliber Browning weapons seem to have been prized acquisitions.

A *Fallschirmjäger* armed with an early-model FG 42 in Normandy, June 1944. The Luftwaffe sought a single *Fallschirmjäger* weapon that would replace the Kar 98k bolt-action rifle, MG 34 squad machine gun, and MP 40 submachine gun, but the FG 42 was never produced in sufficient quantities to make this a reality. (Bundesarchiv, Bild 101I-720-0344-09/ Vennemann, Wolfgang/CC-BY-SA 3.0 DE)

Fallschirmjäger train with a 10cm NbW 35 heavy mortar in France. The NbW 35 was originally intended as a smoke thrower, and a means for delivering chemical weapons. It was replaced in the *Nebelwerfer* units by 10cm and 15cm multiple rocket launchers and the surplus weapons were assigned to *Fallschirmjäger* and *Gebirgsjäger* (mountain troops). Two NbW 35 equipped the mortar platoon of 13./FJR 8 during the battles northeast of Saint-Lô. (michael cremin/Alamy Stock Photo)

Mortars provided indirect firepower, a critical factor in the close countryside of Normandy, and would inflict the majority of Allied casualties during the campaign. There were two types of 8cm mortar used by heavy-weapons companies in *Fallschirmjäger* battalions. The 8cm Granatwerfer 34, the standard infantry mortar, fired a 7lb 11oz bomb to 1.5 miles. Designed for airborne use, the kurzer 8cm Granatwerfer 42 was a shortened version of the 8cm GrW 34; at 58lb the kz GrW 42 weighed less than half of the GrW 34's 137lb, but its maximum range was just 0.7 miles. Fallschirmjäger-Regiment 8 was issued with two 10cm Nebelwerfer 35, a scaled-up version of the 8cm mortar originally intended for projecting chemical weapons; it fired a 16lb 4oz round to a range of 1.9 miles. Fallschirmjäger-Regiment 6 had a company of nine 12cm Granatwerfer 42. This fired a 32lb bomb to 3.7 miles, comparable performance to the US 105mm M3 howitzer.

The Germans developed two handheld antitank weapons. The Panzerfaust 30, introduced in 1943, was a single-shot disposable rocket powered by a gunpowder charge. At 8.8cm, it had a larger caliber than the US Bazooka and could penetrate thicker armor. The Raketenpanzerbüchse 54 or *Ofenrohr* ("Stovepipe") was an enlarged copy of the Bazooka and had a range of about 175yd. Its hollow-charge warhead could penetrate the armor of any Allied tank.

The regimental antitank companies and divisional antitank battalions had heavier weapons. The 7.5cm PaK 40 was the standard antitank gun and could penetrate any tank in US service at ranges up to 1,640yd. Lightweight weapons specially issued to *Fallschirmjäger* included the 4.2cm lePaK 41 and 2.8cm sPzB 41 antitank guns, both of which achieved superior muzzle velocity and penetration courtesy of a squeeze-bore design and special tungsten-core ammunition; a combination that enabled them to penetrate the armor of an M4 medium tank at close range. While production of both types had ceased by 1944 due to difficulties in obtaining tungsten, the 3. Fallschirmjäger-Division seems to have had some on strength.

Regimental *Pionier* (combat engineer) companies and divisional battalions were equipped with flamethrowers as assault weapons. Weighing 62lb, the

Two heavily laden *Fallschirmjäger* with an RPzB 54 *Panzerschreck* anti-tank rocket launcher, Normandy, 1944. The rearmost man wears a standard M35 helmet and is armed with a slung Kar 98k rifle, and both carry stick grenades. The *Panzerschreck* was based on captured American M1 Bazookas. It was a larger, heavier weapon, firing an 8.8cm RPzB Gr 4322 HEAT rocket projectile. (michael cremin/Alamy Stock Photo)

Flammenwerfer 41 projected a mixture of tar and gasoline to a range of 35yd. In 1944, the Germans also introduced the Einstossflammenwerfer 46, a single-shot lightweight flamethrower weighing 8lb that could project a half-second burst of flame to 30yd. It is not clear whether this weapon was used in Normandy.

US Army

The essential weapon of the US infantryman was the .30-caliber M1 Garand semiautomatic rifle, which offered a step increase in aimed firepower compared to bolt-action rifles such as the German Kar 98k. One US soldier in each platoon was issued a .30-caliber M1903 Springfield bolt-action rifle

US soldiers examine the wreckage of a German vehicle that was towing a 7.5cm PaK 40 antitank gun when struck during the aerial bombardment preceding the Allied offensive west of Saint-Lô, July 25, 1944. By this time the PaK 40 was the standard German antitank gun and equipped the *Panzerjäger-Abteilung* of each *Fallschirmjäger* division. It could penetrate the armor of any tank used by the First US Army in July 1944; but like the 57mm M1 antitank gun, it had limited mobility in the hedgerow country. (Photo12/UIG/Getty Images)

A 155mm M1 howitzer in action near Saint-Lô, July 1944. The M1 fired a 96lb shell to 16,000yd. Ammunition included high-explosive, white-phosphorous smoke, and illuminating rounds. A person within 30yd of the point of impact of a high-explosive shell would have a 50 percent chance of receiving an incapacitating wound. Each infantry division had a battalion of 12 M1 howitzers. Further battalions were part of the corps artillery. The M1 had a slower rate of fire than the 105mm M2 howitzer, which fired a 37lb shell. (Photo12/UIG/Getty Images)

to be used for firing rifle grenades or by a sniper. One disadvantage of the M1 – its powder was not smokeless – only became apparent during the campaign in Normandy.

The US Army's squad automatic weapon was the .30-caliber M1918 Browning Automatic Rifle (BAR). This 1918-vintage design used the same .30-06 round as the M1 Garand and had a theoretical rate of fire of 500rd/min, but in reality this was constrained by the limitations of a 20-round magazine.

Issued to platoon commanders and soldiers who needed a weapon for personal protection, the .30-caliber M1 semiautomatic carbine fired a lower-powered .30 round than the M1 Garand. Weighing about twice as much as a .45-caliber M1911 semiautomatic pistol but half as much as an M1 Garand, the M1 carbine was not particularly popular. It lacked smokeless powder, and the catch that held the magazine up into the carbine just would not do so, especially if the weapon was dropped or the user made sudden movements like jumping or falling. Various "field expedients" such as elastic bands, friction tape, string, cord, and even rope were used to hold the magazine in place (Spencer 1984). The .45-caliber Thompson submachine gun, allocated six per company, was used as a close-range automatic weapon in a similar role.

The US Army used the Mk II "pineapple" fragmentation grenade, the Mk III offensive concussion grenade, and the M15 WP (white phosphorus) grenade for screening smoke and antipersonnel actions. Infantry had an effective close-range antiarmor weapon in the form of the 2.36in M1 "Bazooka" antitank rocket launcher, accurate up to 100yd. Antitank companies of US infantry battalions were equipped with the 57mm M1 antitank gun, which could penetrate most German armor likely to be encountered in the US sector apart from the frontal armor of the Panther medium tank.

The two mortars used by the US infantry were the 81mm M1 and the 60mm M2. The M1 had a minimum range of 200yd and could fire a 6lb 14oz M43A1 high-explosive round to a range of 3,290yd and a 10lb 10oz M45 high-explosive round to 2,250yd; WP and illuminating rounds could also be used. The M2, deployed by the infantry company's weapons platoon, could fire high explosive and WP rounds to a minimum range of 220yd and a maximum range of 1,965yd.

The US infantry was backed by the formidable firepower of the US Army's field artillery. Each infantry regiment had a cannon company with six 105mm M3 light howitzers, firing a 37lb 8oz round up to 7,250yd. The cannon company was often affiliated with one of the divisional artillery regiments and acted as an extra fire unit for the divisional artillery group. Each infantry division had four artillery battalions, three with 12 105mm M2 howitzers each and the fourth with 12 155mm M1 howitzers. Additional artillery battalions were added to enhance the divisional artillery group for offensive operations. US Army fire control was very flexible. Calls for fire could be responded to by any artillery in range, even from other divisions. Each artillery battalion had a light observation aircraft – an Aeronca L-3 or Piper L-4 Grasshopper – which would observe and direct artillery fire from the air. This was invaluable in Normandy, where few high vantage points overlooked German-held ground.

The US infantry was also occasionally supported by Allied fighter-bombers. These missions were typically planned at the divisional level, but there were problems using close air support in the *bocage*. It was difficult for aviators to pick out terrain features, and a lack of ground-to-air communications precluded anyone at the company or battalion level from directing air strikes, although targets might be indicated by artillery firing a colored-smoke round.

Lightly kitted US soldiers, one with an M9 Bazooka, take shelter in the *bocage* terrain. The Bazooka was the main antitank weapon available to US forces fighting in the *bocage*, with a minority of infantrymen trained in its use. It had a reputation for unreliability but could penetrate 4in of armor – enough to penetrate the side armor of the Panther medium tanks and *Sturmgeschütze* the US infantry faced. (ullstein bild/ullstein bild via Getty Images)

TACTICS, TRAINING, AND LEADERSHIP

Ultimately, tactics are a matter of the commander's judgment, influenced by doctrine and based on an appreciation of the situation – the mission, the ground, the enemy, friendly forces, etc. There were many similarities between the minor tactics and training of the German *Fallschirmjäger* and their US infantry counterparts. Soldiers were organized into ten-man *Gruppen* (German) or 12-man rifle squads (US Army), each under the command of an NCO and fielding at least one automatic weapon (the German MG 34 or MG 42 or the US BAR). Rifle-squad members were not to bunch together but to remain close enough for the NCO to exercise command over his men. Tactical movement should make use of cover as far as possible and employ fire and movement to get close to the enemy.

There were differences between German and US tactics and training, some of which stemmed from differences in equipment and organization, while others were due to doctrine. In theory, the rifle-squad leader had three rifle teams. There were two pairs of scouts, a three-man BAR team, and a five-man rifle team. The US rifleman's semiautomatic M1 Garand had a higher rate of fire than the German bolt-action Kar 98k, while the German automatic MG 34 and MG 42 had far higher rates of fire than the US BAR. A higher proportion of the US rifle squad's firepower was provided by the M1 Garand, whereas the German *Gruppe*'s firepower was centered on the MG 34 and MG 42. Indeed, German tactical manuals recommended that, in many cases, fire should only be conducted with the machine gun. The US rifle squad was more a squad of riflemen supported by a light automatic weapon, while the German *Gruppe* was built around the light machine gun. The small fields of the *bocage* country, with its limited fields of fire and obstacles to movement, posed more challenges for the US Army, which expected to use armor to support infantry, than for the light infantry of the *Fallschirmjäger*.

US troops man a 57mm M1 antitank gun in Normandy. A British-designed weapon, the M1 was only issued armor-piercing ammunition in US service, thus limiting its antipersonnel effectiveness. The M1 could penetrate German self-propelled guns and the side armor of Panther medium tanks. Weighing 2,679lb, the gun was relatively easy for the six-man detachment to manhandle, but a tractor was usually used for ease of movement. The battalion antitank platoon was equipped with three of these guns. (Boyer/Roger Viollet via Getty Images)

The basic training of both German and US troops was essentially similar. Civilians were turned into soldiers via drill, physical, and small-arms training. US Army training seems to have included much range work, marching, and tactical maneuvers. Before D-Day, the 3. and 5. Fallschirmjäger-Divisionen were deployed in Brittany, and Fallschirmjäger-Regiment 6 was in Normandy, but none of these formations was tasked with the same workload of defensive labor that interrupted training for the Heer units defending the Atlantic Wall. This meant they could continue unit training – and the troops of Fallschirmjäger-Regiment 6 were able to train in the hedgerow country of Normandy.

Fallschirmjäger

The German manual for commanding combined-arms formations was the 1933/34 publication *Truppenführung* ("Troop leading"). While every country published some doctrine for leading formations, the significance of the German doctrine lay in the nuances of the German military culture derived from its 19th-century experience. In the German view, war was inherently chaotic and any attempt by generals to impose order was doomed to failure. The only route to success was to devolve tactical decisions to the lowest level where informed decisions could be made. The doctrine in *Truppenführung* stressed that in circumstances under which the mission could no longer be accomplished, commanders were to use their initiative and inform their superiors of their decision.

The corollary was that commanders should be trained to think two levels higher so that they understand what their superiors were seeking to achieve.

Fallschirmjäger in training are shown the MP 40 submachine gun at Stendal-Borstel airfield. Note the instructor seems to be demonstrating how the weapon should be supported by holding the magazine housing, not the magazine, in order to avoid stoppages. (Weltbild/ullstein bild via Getty Images)

Commanders were taught that quick decisions were essential to take advantage of fleeting opportunities that presented themselves and that every soldier had a duty to undertake aggressive action. The Germans believed that in attack or defense, the commander should decide the main point of effort. This had an impact on how German officers and NCOs were selected and trained. If the regimental commander was to trust the actions of a platoon commander, the junior officer needed to be well trained.

German training for officers and NCOs was thorough and systematic. During World War II, all German officers and NCOs started as private soldiers. Those identified as potential officers and NCOs were appointed as officer candidates and carried out the functions of an NCO for a few months. Those with a higher education certificate might be selected for officer training, which was based on battalion command rather than platoon as in the US Army. Those without the education necessary for officer selection would undergo a ten-week NCO training course. There were proportionately fewer officers in the German than in the US Army. NCOs in the Wehrmacht carried out many tasks carried out by officers in the US Army.

Two smartly dressed *Fallschirmjäger* motorcyclists. Motorcycles were mainly used by liaison officers and messengers. The man in the sidecar appears to be wearing improvised googles. (Keystone-France/Gamma-Rapho via Getty Images)

While much of this doctrine was a matter for higher commanders, it did have an impact on the soldiers struggling on the ground in the *Gruppe* and *Zug* (platoon) – in particular, the level of experience of the NCOs and junior officers. German *Gruppe* tactics were based around the section's MG 34 or MG 42 light machine gun.

German tactical communication equipment was good but not as plentiful as that of the US Army. The Germans had man-pack radios, but nothing like the US handheld "walkie-talkie." The Germans minimized the use of radio communications in forward areas as there was a widespread belief that the Allies could locate the position of radio transmissions with enough accuracy to target the sender. Thus, the Germans made use of telephone lines, light signals, and runners.

US Army

The United States, of course, has its own military style; what Weigley (1960) refers to as "The American Way of War," characterized by a heavy emphasis on logistics, overwhelming material superiority, and an inclination to avoid military or political conflict until a late stage. This has been influenced by the US experience of its own civil wars. There was a belief in putting pressure on an enemy along the whole front and pressing until the enemy gave way. In the US doctrine, the main offensive instrument was the infantry division. This was more optimized for maneuver than the assault, and the bulk of the force's striking power was in the form of indirect firepower.

Field artillery was very effective against exposed troops and soft targets. A battery of four guns would provide a pattern of shell splinters covering roughly a hectare – the size of a football pitch. A well-placed defensive fire could stop an attack or counterattack. Field artillery had limited effects on troops with protection from field defenses, however. An artillery barrage would force defenders to take cover and suppress their return fire. An assault would need to be carefully timed to arrive before the defenders had recovered from the effects of a barrage while minimizing the casualties from friendly fire. This also called for the attacking soldiers to have a high level of confidence in their commanders' judgment.

US doctrine for the tactical handling of an infantry division was set out in FM 100-5 *Field Service Regulations: Operations* (1941). Superficially, this is similar to the German *Truppenführung*, but postwar analysis by a panel of former Wehrmacht officers highlighted some significant differences. By contrast with German doctrine, FM 100-5 encouraged commanders to specify in more detail the actions of subordinates. There was also an emphasis on the offensive and a tendency to formulate approaches for all possible situations that subordinates might face, thus eroding initiative.

US soldiers, their shoulder patches obscured by the censor, move forward in *bocage* terrain. The soldier moving up behind the prone rifle grenadier in the foreground appears to be carrying a Bangalore torpedo explosive charge. It is unlikely that a photographer would accompany an assault, so this photograph might have been taken in one of the tactical schools run by the 2d and 29th Infantry divisions in late June. (Keystone-France/Gamma-Keystone via Getty Images)

MORALE AND MOTIVATION

Fallschirmjäger

An elite force formed from volunteers, the *Fallschirmjäger* fostered a strong collective ethos. The Luftwaffe – and indeed the entire Wehrmacht – were, by 1944 political organizations. Every member of the Wehrmacht had sworn allegiance to Adolf Hitler; and the Luftwaffe, the parent service of the *Fallschirmjäger*, was founded by Göring with a Nazi ethos. There were some ardent Nazis among the *Fallschirmjäger* ranks. Major Friedrich Alpers, who would take over Fallschirmjäger-Regiment 9 after the death of Major Kurt Stephani on August 20, 1944, was a Nazi politician who had served in the *Sturmabteilung* (SA) and *Schutzstaffel* (SS). Indeed, Alpers had the dubious distinction of being temporarily suspended from the SS after complaints of excessive violence.

This pre-1944 image shows a *Fallschirmjäger* MG 34 team demonstrating a change of position. The tripod mounting was awkward and heavy. (ullstein bild/ullstein bild via Getty Images)

An Allied intelligence report noted how the majority of the prisoners of war from the 3. Fallschirmjäger-Division maintained their belief in the Nazi regime and in Germany's ultimate victory. Unlike other elements of the Wehrmacht, the *Fallschirmjäger* continued to regard their officers with respect and admiration, and prisoners were distraught when news of the death of Major Stephani reached them (Graves 2015). While faith

Der Adler
BERLIN, 1. AUGUST-HEFT 1944
Sonderdruck
unverkäuflich
HERAUSGEGEBEN UNTER MITWIRKUNG DES REICHS-LUFTFAHRTMINISTERIUMS

Die wohlverdiente Zigarette
Durch Dreck und Schlamm hat sich der Melder in die vorderste Linie durchgeschlagen. In seinem verkrusteten Gesicht spiegelt sich noch die Anstrengung der letzten Stunden, aber auch die Gelassenheit des Kämpfers, der das unmöglich Scheinende geschafft hat und nun mit leiser Befriedigung an der Zigarette zieht - Typus des deutschen Frontsoldaten, der sich auch den schwierigsten Situationen gewachsen zeigt
PK-Aufnahme Kriegsberichter Erwin Seeger (Wb)

363

in the Führer might explain a belief in a German victory, the quality of the *Fallschirmjäger* leaders made a difference. A *Fallschirmjäger* officer who served in Italy dismissed the accusation that the *Fallschirmjäger* were fanatical Nazis with the observation that the US paratroopers were good soldiers, but no one would attribute their toughness and determination to fanatical supporters of the Democrats.

Dating from August 1944, this image from *Der Adler* ('The Eagle') magazine shows a mud-caked *Fallschirmjäger* lighting a cigarette. (INTERFOTO/Alamy Stock Photo)

A US soldier delivers mail to members of his unit in Saint-Lô, July 1944. Mail from home was seen as key to maintaining the morale of soldiers on operations. (Mondadori via Getty Images)

OPPOSITE
Two US Army medics treat a soldier for a wrist wound sustained in the Saint-Lô area. Not surprisingly, the wounded soldier has a smile on his face, for he is the recipient of a "million-dollar wound" – one that would take him out of the battle, but was unlikely to be a life-changing impairment. (Photo12/UIG/ Getty Images)

US Army

US Army personnel in Normandy were the soldiers of a democracy. Typical comments by veterans are that they were there to do a job and go home. Years after World War II, Sergeant Richard W. Herklotz of the 29th Infantry Division refuted the idea that the Normandy fighting was heroic, noting that he and others were simply doing what their nation wanted them to do; those who survived counted themselves fortunate (Lewis 2014: 299).

The US Army's replacement system and lack of a rotation policy caused problems for unit cohesion. The system was characterized by an industrial approach to the supply of replacements for casualties. A replacement infantryman was treated little differently than a spare part in a machine. Although some units had some form of induction for replacements, there was no systematic program. Furthermore, the pressure on US infantry to undertake offensive operations meant there was often no alternative but to introduce replacements to units in combat.

The replacement, sent to join a group of strangers with a sense of unit pride and cohesion, often had a difficult time adjusting to front-line conditions. Soldiers who joined a unit before it entered combat had the opportunity to become part of a team through many weeks of training. Replacements, unknown to the veterans of their new unit, felt alone in their baptism of fire and typically suffered higher casualty rates in their first engagements than did those units composed entirely of untried soldiers (Steckel 1994).

Hill 192

June 12–July 12, 1944

BACKGROUND TO BATTLE

Generalfeldmarschall Erwin Rommel considered the Allied advance from Caen toward Paris to be the most important threat and therefore this sector should take priority. Despite this, the 7. Armee had identified Saint-Lô as an important crossroads and key to the defense of western Normandy. The II. Fallschirmkorps was ordered to take command of the sector east of Saint-Lô and prepare to drive the Allies into the sea with the 3. Fallschirmjäger-Division, 17. SS-Panzergrenadier-Division *Götz von Berlichingen*, and 352. Infanterie-Division under command.

On D-Day the 3. Fallschirmjäger-Division – the strongest German infantry formation in the West – was in the Rennes area. Its highly motivated paratroopers were well equipped except with artillery and transport. Although designated as a motorized formation, this really meant that, unlike infantry divisions, there was no provision for animal transport. By the end of June 7 the division was on the move. It could muster enough motor transport for a regiment-sized battlegroup composed of one battalion from Fallschirmjäger-Regiment 8 and a second from Fallschirmjäger-Regiment 9, a company of the antitank battalion, two *Pionier* companies, the antiaircraft-artillery battalion, and two artillery batteries, all under command of Major Friedrich Alpers. This battlegroup moved by road during the night of June 6/7 to Avranches then Saint-Lô and deployed northeast to south of the Forêt de Cerisy on June 10–11. The remainder of the division marched on foot, with the aid of hired animal transport and shuttle runs by their limited motor transport. They reached Saint-Lô by June 22, with minimal casualties, having avoided the attention of Allied air forces and French Resistance groups.

Captured US soldiers in Saint-Lô, June 12, 1944. *Fallschirmjäger* and Heer (Army) units had captured several hundred US troops by June 11, including over 100 from 2/115. Prisoners of war on both sides seem to have been reasonably well treated once within the administrative system, though some US accounts (Calder 1949; Spencer 1984) mention *Fallschirmjäger* being ill-treated or shot out of hand. (ullstein bild/ullstein bild via Getty Images)

Generalleutnant Schimpf took personal command of this advanced group. Schimpf had an unusual background for commanding paratroops. He had fought in World War I as an infantry officer and served in the Reichswehr in the 1920s. His interest in aviation led him to join the newly formed Luftwaffe in 1935, obtaining a doctorate in engineering and serving as an engineering staff officer. In 1941 he was appointed to command a newly established Luftwaffe field division, in which role he performed well enough to be entrusted with forming and commanding the 3. Fallschirmjäger-Division.

Rommel's plans to deal with the Allied beachhead in Normandy foresaw the 3. Fallschirmjäger-Division as an attacking force striking north through the Forêt de Cerisy, alongside the armored formations in Panzergruppe West on their eastern flank. Indeed, Schimpf put forward a plan to attack into the Forêt de Cerisy, but this was vetoed by the 7. Armee. After the disruption of the Panzergruppe West plans occasioned by the June 10 air strike on its headquarters, II. Fallschirmkorps was ordered to adopt a defensive pose. According to Schimpf, the battlegroup from the 3. Fallschirmjäger-Division occupied a sector from Saint-Germain-d'Elle to Bérigny to Couvains as a "mere line of combat outposts" (War Dept 1944c). It was only when the bulk of the division arrived after its 220-mile march that the sector could be divided up into independently responsible defensive sectors.

The 2d Infantry Division plan for June 12 was for the 9th Infantry Regiment to capture the high ground south of Littcou. The 23d Infantry Regiment was to secure the high ground around Hill 192, while the 38th Infantry Regiment was in reserve. On June 11, the 23d Infantry, under the command of Colonel Hurley E. Fuller, who had commanded a company in the regiment in combat in 1918, was in an assembly area north of Cerisy-la-Forêt. It was here that the order for the attack on Hill 192 was issued. The 23d Infantry was to pass through the positions of the 38th Infantry with the 1/23 and 2/23 advancing and 3/23 in reserve.

MAP KEY

1   June 10: A mobile battlegroup from the 3. Fallschirmjäger-Division deploys southwest of the Forêt de Cerisy in a line of combat outposts from Saint-Germain-d'Elle to Bérigny and Couvains.

2   June 12: Elements of the 2d Infantry Division cross the Elle River.

3   June 12: The 23d Infantry's attack on Hill 192 unexpectedly meets tough resistance from German airborne forces the Americans had not expected to face.

4   June 13: During the morning, two battalions of the 38th Infantry attack toward Hill 192 through 1/23's positions and penetrate the German defenses almost 2 miles south of the Elle, but run into heavy resistance and pull back after noon.

5   June 16: All three infantry regiments of the 2d Infantry Division attack, with the 38th Infantry to the west, the 23d Infantry on Hill 192, and the 9th Infantry on Saint-Georges-d'Elle, including the support of a platoon of M4 tanks. Bérigny is captured by Co. E, 23d Infantry, then abandoned as US forces make little progress elsewhere.

6   June 19: Supported by a rolling barrage, 1/23 and 3/38's attack on Hill 192 is unsuccessful.

7   June 20: The main body of the 3. Fallschirmjäger-Division arrives and the German defenses are reorganized.

8   July 11–12: After a three-week period of reflection, during which the Americans supplement their infantry firepower, adapt their tanks, and train their forces in infantry–engineer–armor cooperation, attacks by the 23d Infantry and 38th Infantry capture Hill 192.

Battlefield environment

Hill 192 was the highest point on a ridge that stretched 5 miles east-northeast from Saint-Lô to the Elle River. The high ground (sometimes known as the Martinville Ridge) offered an approach to Saint-Lô from the east. Hill 192 provided observation to the north as far as Omaha Beach. The Germans improved the visibility by constructing an observation tower. The Elle, scarcely bigger than a stream, wound its way north and then west of the large, irregular ridge east of Saint-Lô. Northeast of the ridge's eastern edge was the Forêt de Cerisy. The ground sloped down from the forest to the stream and then up to the ridge. The land was *bocage* (hedgerow country), with fields of pasture, orchards, and small woods. The villages of

Saint-Georges-d'Elle and Bérigny were constructed of sturdy Norman stone, as were most buildings of the farms and hamlets every few hundred yards across the area.

The weather in June 1944 was mixed. There were days of low clouds and rain, which prevented Allied fighter-bombers from intervening on the battlefield. The poor weather was good news for the Germans, who could bring up supplies and reinforcements with little fear of Allied air strikes. During June 19–24 a major storm hampered the Allied landings on the Normandy beaches, which resulted in a rationing of artillery ammunition for V Corps.

This image of US soldiers moving along a country road out of contact with the enemy shows the height of the hedge banks and the hedges growing on them. Many of the hedges bordered fields created perhaps a thousand years earlier. The deep sunken lanes were the result of the passage of farm animals and carts over centuries. While there were similar fields in Britain, no special attention could be paid to training in hedgerow country in advance of D-Day for security reasons. (Photo12/UIG/Getty Images)

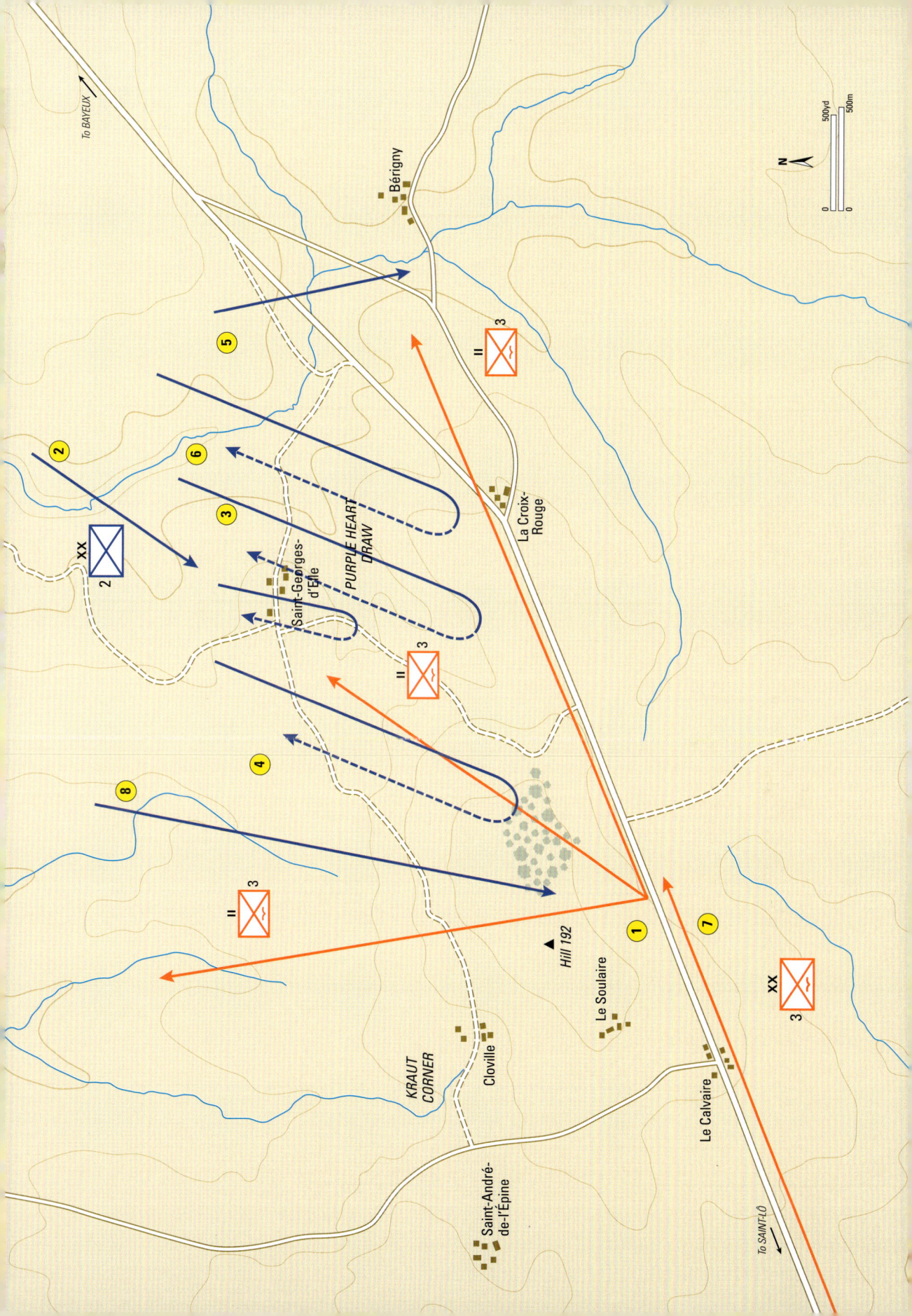

To BAYEUX

Bérigny

500yd
500m

N

⑤

II ☒ 3

② ③ ⑥

XX ☒ 2

La Croix-
Rouge

PURPLE HEART DRAW

Saint-Georges-
d'Elle

II ☒ 3

④

⑧

II ☒ 3

① ⑦

Hill 192

XX ☒ 3

Le Soulaire

Le Calvaire

KRAUT
CORNER

Cloville

Saint-André-
de-l'Épine

To SAINT-LÔ

INTO COMBAT

Regimental orders for the 23d Infantry were given in the assembly area but with no opportunity for reconnaissance. There was no artillery representative at the orders group, nor any representative from the 741st Tank Battalion assigned to support the regiment. The order of march was specified as a column of companies, which in 1/23 was interpreted to mean a column of platoons, while 2/23's companies deployed in skirmish lines.

Both 2/23 and 3/23 ran into ambushes by German units, identified as elements of the 3. Fallschirmjäger-Division, who had been in position for a day or so, and met a similar fate. When 2/23's two assault companies, Co. F and Co. G, reached the hedgerows running generally along the banks of the Elle River, the Germans on the west bank opened fire with small arms and machine guns, supported by antiaircraft guns in the ground role. Despite requests for artillery fires, American attempts to move forward were repulsed by accurate and demoralizing German small-arms and mortar fire "lacing the tops of the hedgerows" (Calder 1949: 13). Any exposed movement along the hedgerows brought some type of enemy fire. By early afternoon, it became apparent that neither battalion could advance any farther, so a defensive line was established about 200yd east of a tributary of the Elle, along the hedgerows that ran parallel to it.

American casualties sustained had been fewer than anticipated or expected from the vigorous defense the Germans had put up to the two battalions' advance. The hedgerows protected the attackers as well as the defenders. The 23d Infantry reported a total of 211 casualties for the day, but there were significant losses among its leaders who had moved forward to spur their riflemen on to the next hedgerow (Spencer 1984).

During June 13–18 the 2d Infantry Division made a series of attacks toward Hill 192 with little ground gained. On June 15 a platoon of tanks was deployed to support an attack on Bérigny, which faltered when the leading tank was knocked out by a *Panzerfaust*, blocking any farther progress. On June 18, an attack by two battalions supported by 20 artillery battalions firing a rolling barrage failed when the infantry lost contact with the barrage. Schimpf wrote of the first few weeks:

> Although the enemy attacked nearly all parts of the line, it was never more than one battalion, and after meeting considerable resistance, he retired to his line of departure. The defence against these attacks, which were like combat patrols, was excellent training, and familiarized the German troops with the enemy's way of fighting. The fact that considerable numbers of enemy tanks were put out of action, mostly by close combat weapons, did away with the tank terror complex. (Meindl & Schimpf 1946)

The outnumbered *Fallschirmjäger* had established a moral superiority over the Americans. The 2d Infantry Division's efforts against this strongpoint had cost the attackers 1,253 casualties. It was readily apparent that, in addition to the natural obstacles presented by the terrain, the previous American attacks on Hill 192 had demonstrated several problems: the US infantry's organic platoon and company weapons lacked the firepower to overcome the enemy;

the Germans seemed to have more automatic weapons; and the Americans found that deploying their tripod-mounted light and medium machine guns in the hedgerows was difficult. Furthermore, the telltale smoke from M1 Garand rifles and BARs was a disincentive for soldiers to fire against an invisible enemy (Stuart 1947). The US Army had plenty of firepower in the form of tanks, but there was a lack of understanding of the tank–infantry relationship.

One approach to the problem developed by the 23d Infantry was of a more determined nature than any previously encountered: the establishment of a rear-area school, with instruction conducted jointly by the regimental executive officer, representatives of the 741st Tank Battalion, and the 2d Engineer Combat Battalion. In this school an effort was made to reemphasize tank–infantry cooperation and mutual interdependence. The training consisted of demonstrations and training in the employment of an improvised tank–infantry–engineer assault team designed to cope with the difficulties of hedgerow warfare. This team consisted of one rifle squad, one engineer demolition detachment of four men, and one medium tank. The engineers were to clear a path for the tank through the hedgerows by placing two satchel charges on a hedgerow and igniting them. Each satchel charge consisted of 20lb of TNT and 11 such charges were carried on each tank. The explosion caused by the two charges would blow a gap in the hedgerow through which a tank could cross without exposing its belly to hostile antitank fire.

An EE-8 field telephone was installed on the rear end of the tank, connected to the intercom system, thereby allowing one of the engineers who walked at the rear of the tank to communicate with the tank commander while the tank was "buttoned-up." The rifle squad received either an extra BAR or a submachine gun, thereby giving two automatic weapons in each squad. One light or medium machine gun was also attached to the squad. The squad was organized so as to provide four scouts, two of whom were armed with BARs or submachine guns.

ABOVE LEFT
The section chief of an American artillery piece in action, June 1944. He wears a second-pattern HBT shirt, deliberately oversized and intended to be worn over other garments. He is holding the telephone connecting the detachment to the command post through which he will receive and acknowledge firing orders. (Photo12/UIG/Getty Images)

ABOVE RIGHT
The crew of an emplaced 60mm M2 mortar in action somewhere in the Saint-Lô sector, summer 1944. Three M2 mortars were in the company weapons platoon, the company commander's own artillery. Mortars were invaluable in the *bocage* terrain, being used to lob bombs over hedgerows to suppress defenders. (Photo12/UIG/Getty Images)

The tactics employed by the tank–infantry–engineer assault team entailed placing the tank and the attached machine gun in position on the friendly side of a hedgerow. The tank fired its 75mm gun into each corner of the hedgerow at the far end of the next field ahead. The machine gun, mounted on a spike in lieu of a tripod and placed on top of the hedgerow, fired bursts covering the breadth of the enemy-held hedgerow. The rifle-squad leader then sent forward the two pairs of scouts, covered by the fire of the tank and the remainder of the rifle squad. One pair of scouts worked along the inner side of each hedgerow perpendicular to the tank's position. When the scouts reached the far corners of the field they tossed over hand grenades to knock out any resistance on the far side of the hedgerow. The two pairs of scouts then converged on the center of the hedgerow in front of the tank's position. The machine gun was then sent forward. Two engineers and the remainder of the rifle squad moved up and selected a new firing position for the tank. The tank moved forward on a telephonic order from an engineer and stopped a short distance in the rear of the new firing site. The engineers placed two satchel charges against the hedgerow and blew a gap in it, thus enabling the tank crew to fire on the next hedgerow in front of the new position. Two riflemen were assigned to protect the tank from antitank teams lying in wait.

On June 28, training started supported by Co. C, 741st Tank Battalion, and Co. C, 2d Engineer Combat Battalion, attached to the 23d Infantry. Nearly all rifle squads in the regiment were given instruction prior to the attack east of Saint-Lô on July 11. Rifle platoons, and in some cases an entire company, were relieved from positions in the line for a half-day of training.

Early in July the First US Army began a series of attacks to secure the high ground east and west of Saint-Lô, which commanded the two corridors through which any Allied attack to the south of Carentan would have to pass. A second objective was to secure vital roads at the base of the Cotentin Peninsula. There would be a succession of attacks from west to east by each of the three corps. VIII Corps started the attack on July 3, followed by VII Corps on July 4. XIX Corps began its attack west of the Vire River on July 7, and on July 11 was joined by the 2d Infantry Division, part of V Corps, in an attack on the high ground east of Saint-Lô.

The remainder of the 3. Fallschirmjäger-Division had arrived by June 17 and took over 15 miles of frontage, from Bérigny to Saint-Lô, with, from west to east, Fallschirmjäger-Regiment 8, Fallschirmjäger-Regiment 5, and Fallschirmjäger-Regiment 9. The two battalions of the advance group were withdrawn into reserve. Over the next two weeks the 3. Fallschirmjäger-Division established more substantial defenses across its sector, digging deep dugouts with overhead protection and firing posts into and through hedgerows.

The field order of the 2d Infantry Division, received on July 7 by the 23d Infantry, gave the 38th Infantry on the right (west) the mission of taking Hill 192 proper, with two battalions in the assault. The 9th Infantry on the left (east) was ordered to support the attack with all available fires. The 23d Infantry, with 1/23 and 3/23, was tasked to take the southeastern slopes of Hill 192 and secure the Bérigny–Saint-Lô highway from the right (west) of its zone through La Croix-Rouge. During the initial stages, 2/23 – less Co. E, attached to the 9th Infantry – was to cover the attack by fire only and move on La Croix-Rouge after 1/23 had secured its objective. The artillery preparation for the attack was scheduled to begin 20 minutes before H-hour with the fires of 12 field-artillery battalions and a chemical-mortar battalion. The infantry were to be supported in the attack by the 741st Tank Battalion.

Throughout the entire July 1–10 period, American patrols were unable to secure any new unit identifications. The enemy was content to improve his defensive positions and "maintained a tight defense against our patrol activities. Friendly patrols invariably met instant fire upon closing with the German outpost positions" (Mildren 1947: 5). US intelligence sections prepared 1:10,000-scale maps showing every hedgerow, sunken road, building, and trail in the area. Code numbers were assigned to each field so that US troop dispositions, as well as enemy locations, could be accurately reported. Intensive reconnaissance was carried on by all American commanders during the days preceding the attack. Rifle-platoon leaders made reconnaissance flights in liaison aircraft, to gain a clearer picture of the ground over which they would attack and to assist them in orienting their units. Every effort was made to provide reliable wire communication for the attack. Wherever tank routes crossed wire lines, linemen went out and dug the lines 1–2ft underground. Line-construction crews also used French commercial telephone poles to keep the lines off the ground in the vicinity of the line of departure. Tanks were infiltrated individually and at one-hour intervals during the hours of darkness on July 9 and 10.

Between 0030hrs and 0300hrs on July 11 the Germans laid down one of the heaviest concentrations of mortar and artillery fire the 2d Infantry Division had experienced. On the American left (east), 2/23 received most of the fire, but the men were so well dug-in that few casualties were incurred, although some were inflicted among tank crews while mounting their tanks (Mildren 1947).

Beginning at 0400hrs, 1/23 and 3/23 quietly moved back 200yd from the positions they had occupied for the past three weeks. This movement was necessary prior to the US artillery preparation because in most cases the German positions were not more than 100yd away. At 0539hrs the scheduled air strike on the objective by four groups of fighter-bombers was canceled due to bad flying weather. One minute later, the artillery barrage began with a tremendous volume of shells landing simultaneously on the enemy positions. For 20 minutes the US soldiers waiting to attack listened to their powerful artillery support as 12 field-artillery battalions, a battalion of 4.2in chemical mortars, and two cannon companies fired on Hill 192 (Little 1947).

At 0600hrs, moving closely behind a scheduled rolling barrage and employing the tank–infantry–engineer assault-team tactics they had previously rehearsed, the American assault companies encountered only moderate resistance in the first few fields. Then the real fighting began as the *Fallschirmjäger* recovered from the initial shock of the artillery preparation. During the latter part of the afternoon, the supporting tanks of Co. C, 741st Tank Battalion, ran low on fuel and ammunition. Resupply was accomplished by the tanks working in relays. At 1730hrs the leading platoon of Co. B had almost reached the Bérigny–Saint-Lô highway and the remainder of 1/23 was echeloned to the left rear along the road leading southwest from Saint-Georges-d'Elle. A-half-hour later, Co. K was attached to 1/23 and Co. A was attached to 3/23.

Hill 192, July 11, 1944

This platoon from 23d Infantry have trained with the tank, which has been modified with two 4in iron pipes fixed to the final drive casing, allowing the tank to force its way through the hedge bank or leave holes in the bank that will hold explosive charges laid by a team of combat engineers.

Besides the BAR, the squad sergeant has a Thompson submachine gun and an M1919 machine-gun team from the heavy-weapons platoon. This squad is supported by ample firepower to suppress the German defenders beyond the next hedgerow.

A smartly dressed *Fallschirmjäger* MG 34 team ready their tripod-mounted weapon for firing. The absence of helmet camouflage and scrim suggests that this photograph was taken in a training environment away from the front. With its long range and devastating crossfire the MG 34 was a fearsome weapon. (GRANGER – Historical Picture Archive/Alamy Stock Photo)

The US regimental commander, Colonel Jay B. Loveless, gave the order to "button up" for the night at 1950hrs and all companies prepared hasty defenses on the positions they had reached. Having gained approximately 1,500yd on the US right (west), 1/23 was dug-in 400–600yd from the Bérigny–Saint-Lô highway. Three officers and 104 enlisted men were wounded in action during the day, while 14 enlisted men were killed in action.

The division field order on July 12 assigned the 23d Infantry the same objective and zones on July 12 as on the preceding day. The time of attack was set at 1100hrs and the line of departure was to be the line presently held by the forward elements of 1/23. At 1100hrs, 1/23 attacked with Co. B on the right (west) and Co. C echeloned to the left rear. At 1115hrs, Co. B crossed the Bérigny–Saint-Lô highway and at 1140hrs the company commander announced that he was on the objective. Co. C, encountering only slight resistance, reached the objective at 1300hrs and Co. K was moved into Co. C's

former position along the Saint-Georges-d'Elle road. At 1415hrs, Co. K was committed in the direction of La Croix-Rouge, attacking across the ground between "Purple Heart Draw" and the Bérigny–Saint-Lô highway, an area the Germans had successfully defended on July 11. The resistance to this attack was so weak that Co. K secured its objective in just two hours.

In the meantime, 2/23 and 3/23 had sent out patrols to ascertain the *Fallschirmjäger* strength and dispositions in the pocket between La Croix-Rouge, Bérigny, and Saint-Georges-d'Elle. At 1700hrs a patrol from Co. F reported that it had successfully made contact with Co. K in La Croix-Rouge. With the agreement of the division commander, Major General Walter M. Robertson, Loveless immediately ordered 2/23 to secure positions astride the highway

between Bérigny and La Croix-Rouge. Moving out around 1800hrs, 2/23 occupied its objective without meeting any resistance, although some casualties were suffered en route when the leading elements ran into a heavily mined area. Meanwhile, 3/23 was ordered into a position north of 1/23 and prepared to relieve that battalion on order. Five officers and 34 enlisted men were wounded in action on July 12, while four enlisted men were killed in action.

The Germans redeployed. The greater part of a battalion from Fallschirmjäger-Regiment 5 had been cut off by the American penetrations; these German elements withdrew, bringing their wounded with them.

Two *Fallschirmjäger* in a camouflaged motor vehicle, Normandy, summer 1944. The Allies had air superiority and their fighter-bombers were a significant threat to which the individual *Fallschirmjäger* had no response other than to seek cover. Fortunately for the Germans, the weather in June and July 1944 was among the wettest on record, which meant Allied plans to use air power were often frustrated by the weather. (Scherl/ Süddeutsche Zeitung Photo/ Alamy Stock Photo)

A member of a US patrol taking cover from enemy sniper activity raises a helmet on an M1 carbine in an effort to reveal the sniper's location, while the remainder of the patrol keeps watch along the road. Note the abandoned MG 42 machine gun in the foreground. (Mondadori via Getty Images)

A *Fallschirmjäger* armed with an early-model FG 42 battle rifle in Normandy, June 21, 1944. The select-fire FG 42 was chambered for the standard 7.92×57mm Mauser cartridge, as the Luftwaffe rejected the "intermediate" 7.92×33mm cartridge being developed. This FG 42 appears to have a 20-round magazine, which limited the weapon's sustained-fire capabilities while making it somewhat unbalanced. The muzzle brake and buffered stock reduced recoil effectively, but the bipod fitted to the early version was positioned too far back from the muzzle, an issue remedied with the late-model FG 42. (Bundesarchiv, Bild 101I-720-0344-11/Vennemann, Wolfgang/CC-BY-SA 3.0 DE)

The 2d Infantry Division had accomplished its mission in two days and was now astride the Bérigny–Saint-Lô highway. It remained in this position until July 26. Measured in terms of the preceding attacks in June, this two-day offensive had been very successful. The Germans had resisted the attack on Hill 192 and Saint-Georges-d'Elle with all the means at their disposal. In addition to elements already in the line, Fallschirm-Sturmgeschütz-Brigade 12, elements of Fallschirm-Aufklärungs-Abteilung 12, and, finally, Fallschirm-Pionier-Bataillon 3 had been committed in a desperate effort to hold the ground.

The German paratroopers had lived up to their reputation as elite troops. There was no coordinated attempt to withdraw and the *Fallschirmjäger* remained in position until destroyed or forced to surrender. A total of 21 prisoners of war were taken on July 11, but only three on July 12. One of these prisoners stated that he had no chance to withdraw because he had been trapped between American artillery fire to his rear and the assaulting troops to his front. A letter taken from a dead *Fallschirmjäger* a few weeks later reveals the impact of the battle:

> We were put in the line East of St Lo. At that time our company strength was 170. Then the 11 of July arrived and the most terrible day of my life. At 0500 our Co. sector got such a dense hail of arty and mortar fire, that we knew a big attack was coming. In addition to that we could hear the rumblings of tanks. At 0530 the firing increased and the tanks moved closer. The hedgerows helped us to hide somewhat from the tanks but they shot right through the rows as through cake dough. At 1000 the order came to withdraw as the position could not be held. I tried to carry my wounded comrade with the help of another soldier but a shell landed a few yards away and wounded him again and also hit the third fellow. On our way back we were covered again with terrific artillery fire. Every moment I expected to get hit. At that moment I lost my nerves. I chewed up a cigarette, bit into the ground and acted like a madman. The others acted just like me. When one hears for hours the whining, whistling and bursting of shells and the moaning and groaning of the wounded one does not feel too well. Our company had only 30 men left. (V Corps Intelligence report, quoted in Mildren 1947)

Clearing the way to Saint-Lô

June 12–July 18, 1944

BACKGROUND TO BATTLE

The 29th Infantry Division was a National Guard formation the three regiments of which had famous antecedents: the 115th Infantry Regiment claimed a lineage to the Maryland Militia, raised in 1775; the 116th Infantry Regiment was part of the Virginia National Guard, its lineage including the Stonewall Brigade of the American Civil War; and the 175th Infantry Regiment was the Baltimore "Dandy 5th." The 116th Infantry was one of the assault regiments on Omaha Beach on D-Day and suffered the heaviest losses.

An M10 tank destroyer near Saint-Lô. The M10 was based on the M4 medium-tank chassis but mounted a slightly bigger 3in (76.2mm) gun than the M4's 75mm gun in a lightly armored open-top turret. M10s would accompany attacking infantry to protect against enemy armor and were widely used as assault guns in the absence of tanks. Twelve M10s from the 821st Tank Destroyer Battalion were part of the task force that made a dash to Saint-Lô on the morning of July 18. (US Signal Corps/Wikimedia/ Public Domain)

The divisional commander was Major General Charles H. "Uncle Charlie" Gerhardt, a controversial commander and hard-driving martinet with obsessions about trivial details such as buckling up helmet chinstraps and cleaning jeeps. His own jeep was said to have been washed five times a day. He was a good trainer but drew criticism for his callous attitude toward casualties. He was said by veterans of the 29th Infantry Division to be a corps commander, with one division in the field, a second in the hospitals, and a third in the cemetery. He would visit at least one of the division's battalions daily. The only forewarning might be Gerhardt's dog, a mutt called "D-Day," which was the recipient of the only emotional warmth expressed by the otherwise buttoned-up Gerhardt.

Gerhardt's assistant divisional commander was Brigadier General Norman D. "Dutch" Cota, Gerhardt's West Point classmate, former staff-college instructor, and part of the D-Day planning team. Cota was one of the most senior US officers to come ashore on D-Day; his actions on Omaha Beach, rallying the confused, frightened, and shell-shocked troops and leading the initial advance, were rewarded with the Distinguished Service Cross and the British Distinguished Service Order and coined several immortal battlefield quotes, including "Anyone who stays on this beach is going to die. Come inland and die there." and "Rangers lead the way." His jeep was named "Fire and Movement." Cota could be found tagging along on some of the more dubious or dangerous divisional operations.

In the ten days after D-Day the 29th Infantry Division cleared the coast west of Omaha Beach and then became the westernmost of the three infantry divisions (1st, 2d, 29th) of V Corps as it pressed inland, against the battered German 352. Infanterie-Division. Not everything went smoothly for the Americans, however. One operation to secure bridges over the Vire was described by Cota as "ill-conceived, ill-planned and ill-executed" (Balkoski 2005). By June 11, the 352. Infanterie-Division withdrew south of the Elle. Despite injunctions from the First US Army commander, Lieutenant General

A determined looking *Fallschirmjäger* armed with an MP 40 submachine gun. The MP 40 was associated in many Allied minds with the *Fallschirmjäger*, though only two were issued to each *Gruppe*. US infantrymen referred to MP 40s as "Burp guns." Its effective range was 100–200yd, which was ample for hedgerow fighting. (INTERFOTO/Alamy Stock Photo)

Omar N. Bradley, to go on the defensive while priority was given to the capture of Cherbourg, Gerhardt and the XIX Corps commander, Major General Charles H. "Cowboy Pete" Corlett, were keen to push as far south as possible. Gerhardt was determined to seize Saint-Lô, 11 miles inland from the Elle. On June 13, the 29th Infantry Division captured its first German paratrooper, one of the advance party of the 3. Fallschirmjäger-Division from Brittany, which took up position east of the 352. Infanterie-Division.

On June 6 the 3. Fallschirmjäger-Division was based in western Brittany. Its soldiers were volunteers from across the Luftwaffe, built around a cadre of experienced NCOs and officers, many wearing cuff titles and decorations associated with battles for Narvik, Crete, Tunisia, Sicily and Monte Cassino. The 3. Fallschirmjäger-Division was a much newer outfit than the 29th Infantry Division, only formed in November 1943, and was the last German airborne formation whose men received jump training.

1 **June 12:** The 29th Infantry Division closes with the Elle River.

2 **June 17:** US forces advance to "Purple Heart Hill" and the Bois de Brétel, creating the Villiers-Fossard salient.

3 **June 22:** The main body of the 3. Fallschirmjäger-Division arrives and the German defenses are reorganized.

4 **June 29:** The 3d Armored Division's CCA attacks German forces in the Villiers-Fossard salient, eliminating it at a heavy cost in American lives.

5 **July 11:** Stosstruppe Kersting, composed of four companies of Fallschirmjäger-Regiment 9, attacks 1/115 and is repulsed with heavy losses on both sides.

6 **July 11:** Despite suffering heavy losses, 1/115 advances.

7 **July 11:** The 116th Infantry uses "one squad, one tank, one field" tactics.

8 **July 13:** The 3. Fallschirmjäger-Division withdraws closer to Saint-Lô.

9 **July 13:** Two battalions of the 175th Infantry deploy south of the Saint-Lô–Bayeux highway (D972).

10 **July 14:** Advancing beyond the American front line, 2/116 becomes a "Lost Battalion." West of the Isigny highway, the 35th Infantry Division takes Hill 122.

11 **July 16:** German forces supported by self-propelled guns launch counterattacks on either side of 2/116's positions, but make no progress.

12 **July 17:** Major Howie's 3/116 infiltrates to 2/116 but makes no further progress following his death.

13 **July 17–18:** 2/115 infiltrates to La Planche.

14 **July 18:** The 3. Fallschirmjäger-Division withdraws south of Saint-Lô.

15 **July 18:** Task Force C enters Saint-Lô with 1/115.

Battlefield environment

This battlefield was the western half of the Martinville Ridge, which extended from Saint-Lô to Saint-Georges-d'Elle. It was the classic Normandy hedgerow country of small fields divided by high hedgerows on banks. Numerous spot heights indicated on the map and mentioned in after-action reports can be hard to find on the ground, but only Points 192 and 122 had tactical significance. Any minor differences in the topography were obscured by the vegetation. From the combatants' point of view, the only terrain that mattered was the field they were in and the next.

The weather in June and July 1944 was typical of a north European summer. Several low-pressure weather systems swept across Normandy, including the Great Storm of June 19–24. Frequently poor weather over the airfields in Britain and France and the target areas prevented Allied aircraft from supporting the 29th Infantry Division. The hedgerow country provided cover for both attackers and defenders alike, as recognized by some US officers: "There is little terrain, however, be it ever so favorable to the enemy, that does not afford the same compensating advantages" (Van der Voert 1947).

The Americans had excellent large-scale maps based on aerial reconnaissance photographs. The Germans lacked detailed mapping, however, and prized captured American maps. One limitation to the American maps was that they did not differentiate between single hedges and double hedges enclosing tracks and noted all as hedgerows – a fact that enabled the Germans to disguise some of their tactical movements.

Typical Normandy hedgerow terrain: a patchwork of fields and orchards separated by high hedgerows. (US Army)

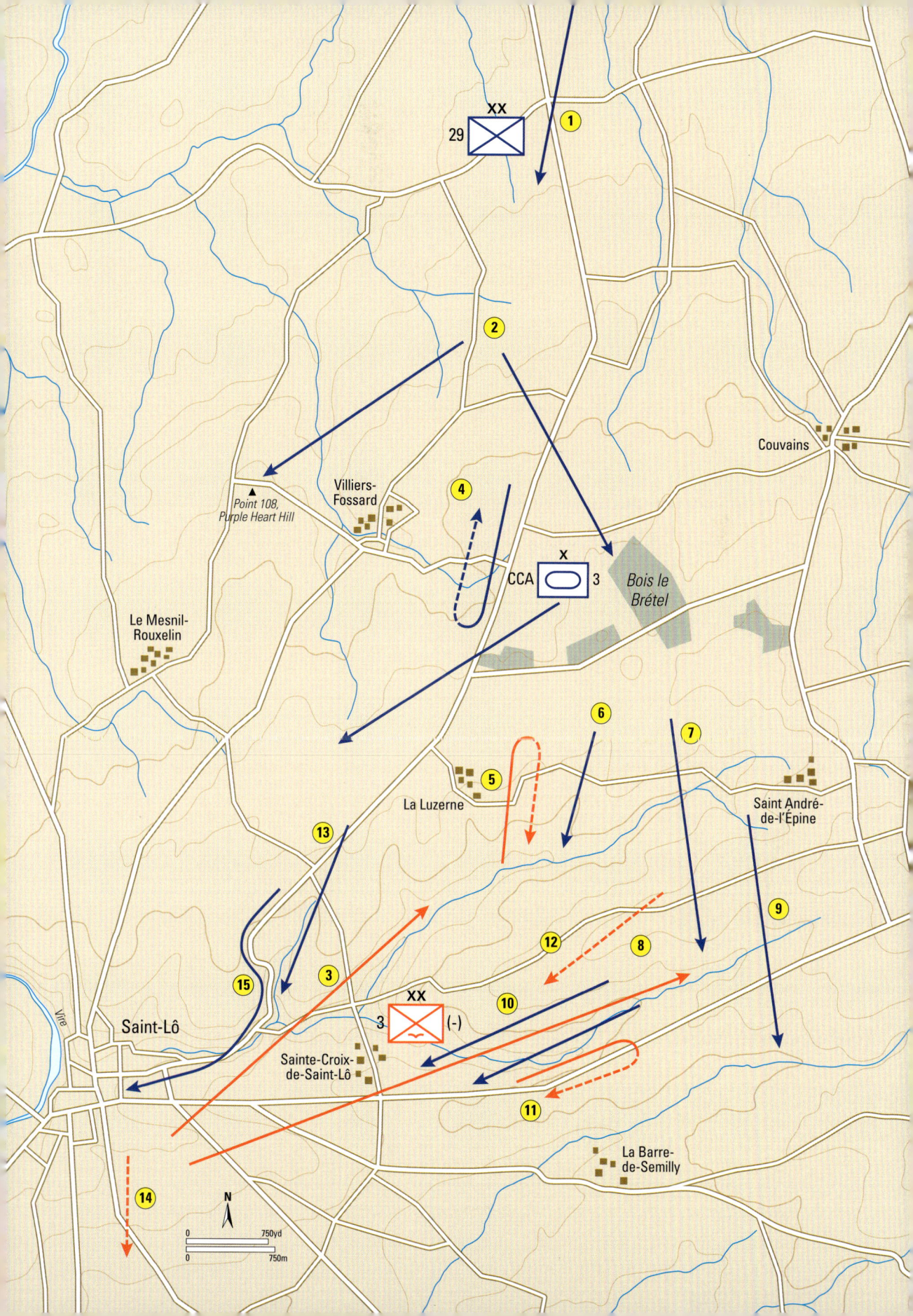

29

XX

①

②

Couvains

④

Villiers-
Fossard

▲ Point 108,
Purple Heart Hill

CCA ◯ 3

*Bois le
Brétel*

Le Mesnil-
Rouxelin

⑥

⑦

⑤

La Luzerne

Saint André-
de-l'Épine

⑬

⑨

⑫

⑧

⑮

③

⑩

Saint-Lô

XX
3 ⌇ (-)

⑪

Sainte-Croix-
de-Saint-Lô

La Barre-
de-Semilly

Vire

N

⑭

0   750yd
0   750m

INTO COMBAT

The 29th Infantry Division's move toward Saint-Lô started on June 12 with the crossing of the Elle. German defensive doctrine called for a main battle line with an outpost line in advance. The *Fallschirmjäger* lacked the plethora of portable radios available to the US troops, instead relying on telephones and runners. Communication difficulties in the *bocage* meant the German outpost line was rarely more than one or two hedgerows in front of the main defensive line. German doctrine was aggressive. Units would make a *Gegenstoss* ("counter-storm") as soon as possible with their own resources to recover any lost ground. Quick counter-storms, even by a few soldiers, would often catch an attacker disorganized before he could consolidate, precipitating a flight to the rear or causing delay.

On June 16, the 29th Infantry Division resumed the attack using a complicated plan that involved battalions leapfrogging each other. *Fallschirmjäger* infiltrated Saint-Clair-sur-l'Elle along an abandoned trench, after 2/116 moved out of the town and before Co. E could move in, resulting in a daylong fight for the town. This was typical of the *Fallschirmjäger* response to American advances. Although heavily outnumbered, small groups of Germans carried out aggressive counterattacks; by the end of June 16, the soldiers of the 29th Infantry Division were barely holding their positions, far short of the gains that Gerhardt had hoped for (Balkoski 2005).

Lieutenant Colonel Glover S. Johns, Jr., commanding 1/115, subsequently noted that combat, even during hard-fought battles, consists of numerous individual actions spread in some cases over several hours (Johns 2002: 173–74). With individual riflemen taking cover, artillery and mortar observers selecting vantage points for observation, and leaders moving around the battlefield as they assessed where and how best to act, combat could be drawn out. Some of the time, there would appear to be little activity, with few shots being fired, but this was indicative of both sides being cautious and unwilling to reveal their own positions by firing. Also, it took time for officers and NCOs to form a view and relay their orders. Even when a course of action had been decided, it took time to implement the plan, especially where preliminary artillery fires were required and soldiers had to move forward cautiously. Actions came to a close either when one combatant sensed an opportunity to press a large, concerted attack, or when the leader of the weaker side decided to pull his forces back.

Sergeant John Robert "Bob" Slaughter of Co. D, 116th Infantry, had a more jaundiced view of combat, noting the appalling smell of corpses, the squalor of 42 days without changing underwear, the early-morning start of each day's fighting, the unremitting hedgerow fighting, and the incorporation of poorly trained replacements. According to PFC Robert L. Sales of Co. B, 116th Infantry, GIs never got used to combat; the threat of German patrols meant few soldiers got much sleep, getting drenched in the rain and existing on cold rations (Kershaw 2003: 181).

There was a pause in the 29th Infantry Division's offensive operations between June 18 and July 11. On June 29, the 3d Armored Division's Combat Command A launched an attack to pinch out a salient at Villiers-Fossard, gaining 550yd at a cost of 31 tanks and over 400 US casualties. Leutnant

Helmut "Bollo" Bollmann, a platoon commander in Fallschirm-Panzerjäger-Abteilung 3, found himself faced by a tank coming directly for his slit trench and feared it would grind him into the ground. He waited until the tank approached close enough for him to be in the dead zone of the tank's vision, leapt out of the trench, in the spirit of close-quarter tank-fighting doctrine, ran round the back of the tank, climbed on the back and disabled the vehicle with a grenade (Way 2019: 130–31).

During the lull in the fighting, the 29th Infantry Division carried out combined-arms training at a regimental training area under Cota's direction. The concept was "one squad, one tank, one field." A four-man team of engineers would accompany each tank to blow holes in the hedges made by two steel prongs welded to the front of each tank. This would be put to the test in a combined attack by 2d Infantry Division on Hill 192 and 29th Infantry Division on the summit of the Martinville Ridge to the west of Hill 192. The attack would be mounted by the 116th Infantry, reinforced with tanks and engineers, on a 1,315yd frontage, with one battalion up and two in reserve. To the right (west), the 115th Infantry on a 5,475yd frontage would mount a holding attack with all three battalions in line, and overlooked on the right by Hill 122, west of the Saint-Lô–Villiers-Fossard–Isigny road, the D191.

On July 11, the 116th Infantry attacked using the "one squad, one tank, one field" tactics. The first 500yd were slow and bloody, but once Hill 192 fell to the 23d Infantry and the 2d Infantry Division moved forward on the left (east), the Germans started to pull back and by the end of the day the 116th Infantry had advanced 3,000yd, with one battalion astride the ridge-top road and two on the far, southern side of the ridge.

On the 115th Infantry front, things had not gone so well. Starting around 0130hrs on July 11, a counterattack mounted by two companies of II./FJR 9, led by Oberleutnant Werner Kersting and aided by a mortar and artillery barrage, struck Johns' 1/115 and penetrated between the widely spaced rifle companies to hit the supporting mortars. The Germans moved back and forth along the road, throwing grenades into the American foxholes (Johns 2002: 136). A platoon leader in Co. B, Lieutenant Fletcher W. Harris, was lying in a foxhole when a German stick grenade suddenly landed by his side. He snatched it up to throw it back over the hedge, but it exploded and severed his right hand (Balkoski 2005). Some of the Americans fled, but the remainder stayed in their foxholes. About a platoon's-worth of soldiers from Co. A who had retreated rallied near 1/115's mortars and fought off the Germans who had penetrated that far into the American position.

Initially, Johns had communication problems: only at 0200hrs was radio contact established with the US artillery, and fire was brought down on

An M38 *Fallschirmjäger* rimless helmet. This was unique to *Fallschirmjäger* and had little similarity with the standard German *Stahlhelm*. The design was intended to provide protection from impact with the ground as well as shrapnel and bullets. There were no projections that might snag with rigging. Inside the helmet is a leather liner, ventilated with holes and held in position by an aluminum band, backed with resilient rubber padding. (World of Triss/Alamy Stock Photo)

the Germans. It took the American troops until 0500hrs to fight off the attackers, supported by US artillery firing defensive fires. During the action, 1/115 suffered more than 100 killed and wounded, while the Germans left 87 bodies in their positions. It was 1130hrs before 1/115 was resupplied with ammunition and the depleted battalion was ready to advance.

The squads and platoons of the assault echelon slipped quietly through the hedgerow, and started at a run for the one on the far side. One platoon with a more aggressive leader leapt the hedge at a charge. They all met the same reception – fire from rifles, machine guns, and submachine guns. Concentrated US fire on one part of the German line proved too much for the *Fallschirmjäger*. Co. B moved quickly through the gap in the German defenses. Each US company reached one hedgerow and then stopped (Johns 2002: 136). The Germans maneuvered against 1/115's open right flank, and the battalion was starting to take casualties. As apathy set in among the GIs and their officers and they focused on digging in rather than trying to press the attack, Johns himself found that his drive to win was flagging (Johns 2002: 136).

Two staff officers – the regimental executive officer and the divisional chief of staff – then appeared. The latter, Colonel Edward H. McDaniel, persuaded Johns to make one last effort. Johns later wrote that he could not recall the details of the afternoon and early evening of July 11, only that he urged his company commanders to make progress. Identifying a weak spot in the German defenses facing Co. B, Johns ordered an artillery strike on a 100yd stretch of enemy-held hedgerow, after which Co. B were able to move through the gap and the *Fallschirmjäger* were prompted to withdraw. It had taken all day for 1/115 to take 500yd of ground, but they had beaten the Germans twice in 24 hours (Johns 2002: 136).

Without detracting from 1/115's courage and tenacity, Johns' attack coincided with Major Stephani's decision to pull Fallschirmjäger-Regiment 9 back to a new defensive position closer to Saint-Lô after the loss of Hill 192 and the 116th Infantry's penetration of his positions. This was a difficult moment for the Germans. One battalion of Fallschirmjäger-Regiment 5 was cut off, but fought its way back to the new German lines, bringing all of its wounded with it.

The following days saw the 29th Infantry Division seeking to drive southwest along the Martinville Ridge with the 116th Infantry and 175th Infantry while the 115th Infantry made diversionary attacks. Limited progress was made by the Americans, however, and the troops on the Martinville Ridge came under fire from the next ridge south. By the end of July 13 the troops were exhausted. The 29th Infantry Division might capture Saint-Lô within a week or so at this rate of advance, but would run out of troops first. July 14 was a rest day and some units were taken out of the line for the day. Gerhardt used the day to drop in unexpectedly on some battalions. His message was that the division had fought well so far, but the battle was not over. Gerhardt's most characteristic action of the day was to tell his aide to pass a message to all battalion commanders that all dead animals in their sector were to be buried.

The attack resumed on July 15 with the added advantage that the 35th Infantry Division on the 29th Infantry Division's right was now

A heavily camouflaged PaK 40 manned by *Fallschirmjäger* in Normandy, 1944. (Imwar/Alamy Stock Photo)

responsible for capturing Hill 122, which it secured that day. As usual the Germans gave up the front-line hedgerows, and withdrew to a main defensive line one or two hedges farther back. During the day, divisional headquarters became convinced that the Germans were at breaking point, and Gerhardt prepared a message for the regimental and battalion commanders calling for an all-out attack to start at 1930hrs and ending his message with the exhortation to fix bayonets. This did not match the fighting on the front line, however. The 115th Infantry lost 119 casualties, including 20 dead, for the gain of 600yd. Despite Gerhardt's exhortation, the 116th Infantry and 175th Infantry on the ridge had made little progress. A bitterly disappointed Gerhardt called off the attack at nightfall (Balkoski 2005).

Unknown to divisional headquarters, however, the Germans on the Martinville Ridge had given way just before night fell. Both 1/116 and 2/116 had made significant advances, with the latter, under Major Sidney V. Bingham, Jr., having advanced to a little village called La Madeleine within 1 mile of Saint-Lô, and become isolated.

Although July 16 was a rest day, ordered by XIX Corps, the 116th Infantry and 175th Infantry had little opportunity to recuperate and reorganize, because the Germans infiltrated through the wide gaps between US Army units on the Martinville Ridge and hit the Americans with a powerful counterattack, supported by *Sturmgeschütze*. One of the assault guns caused consternation to Co. A, 116th Infantry, which had lost its bazooka team. Sergeant Harold E. Peterson, who had assumed command after all six of the company's officers had become casualties during the past week, loaded his M1 Garand with antitank grenades and hit the assault gun six times, forcing it to withdraw (Balkoski 2005).

Unaccountably, Bingham's isolated 2/116 was left more or less alone on July 16, with only sporadic fire from the south, east, and west; with just one aid man, on July 17 the Americans were glad to capture a German medic who was put to work tending to the wounded (Balkoski 2005).

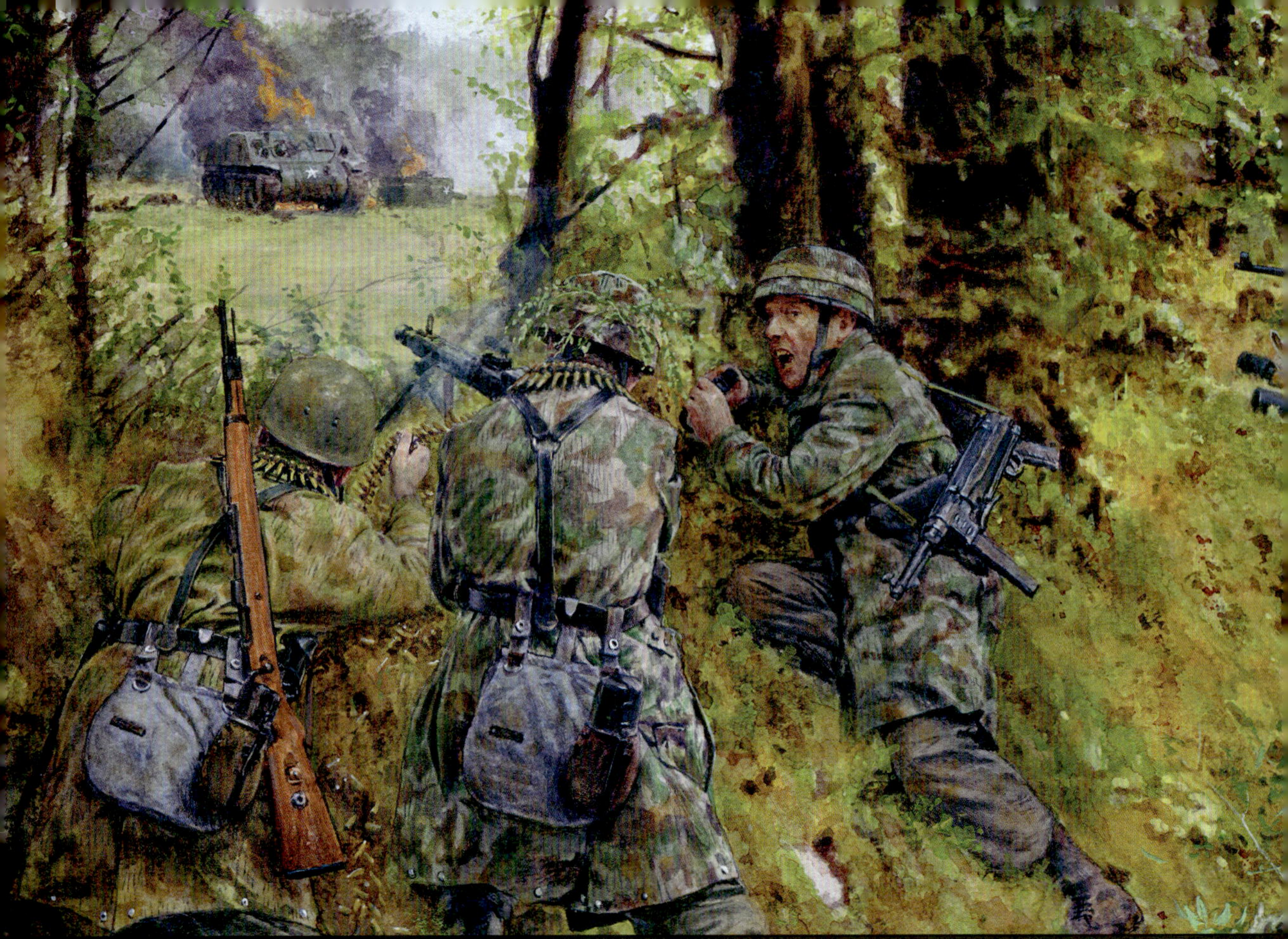

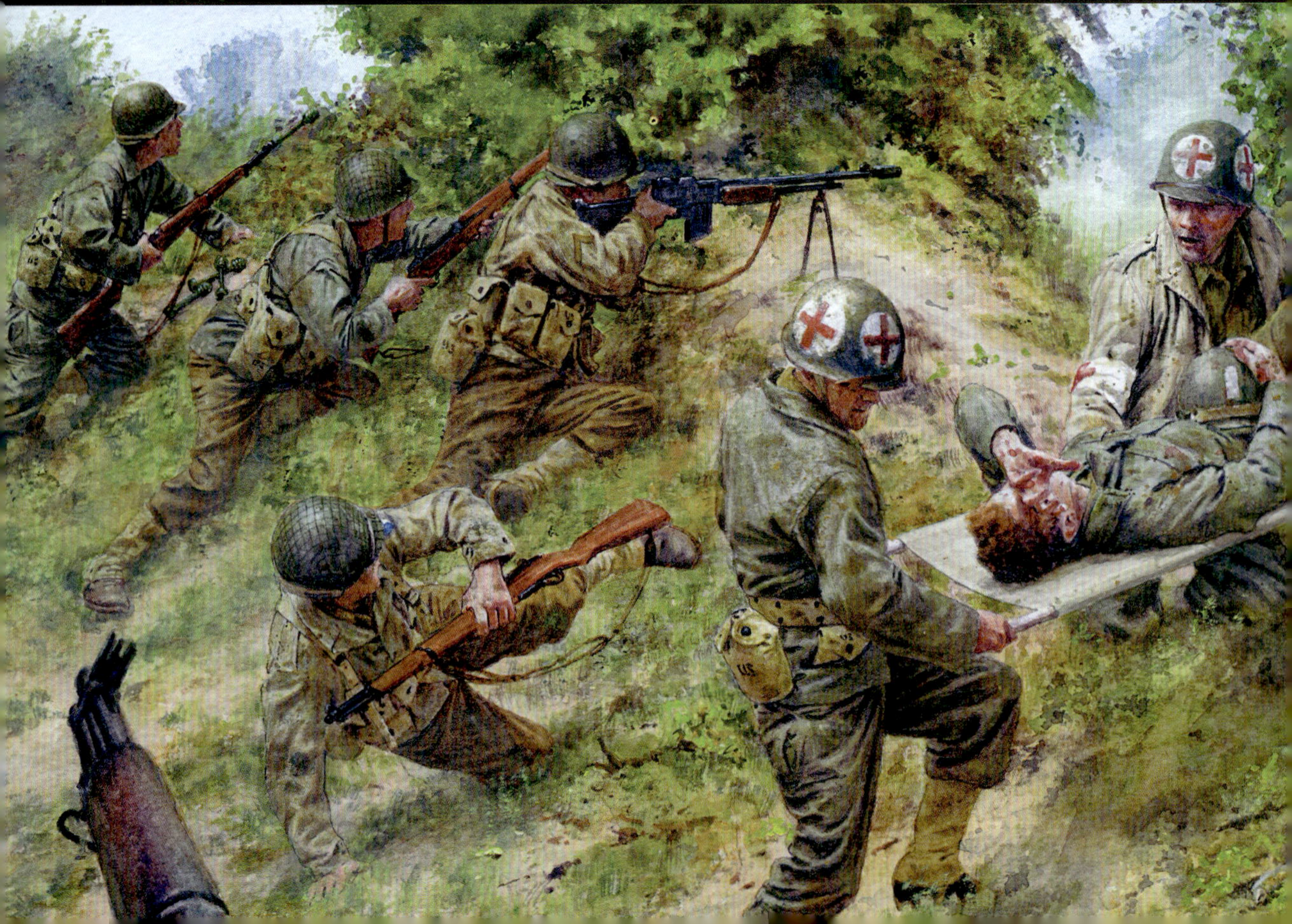

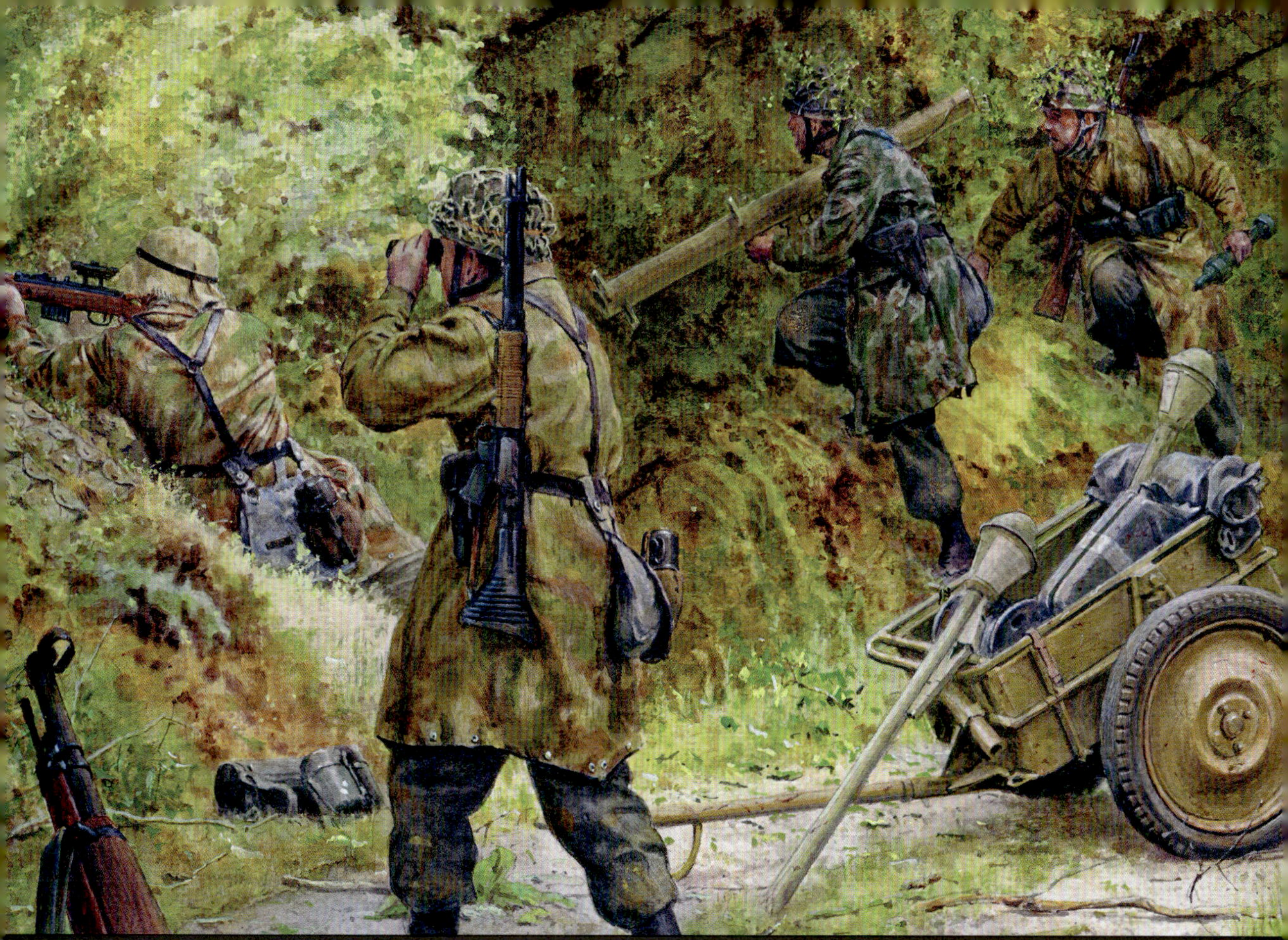
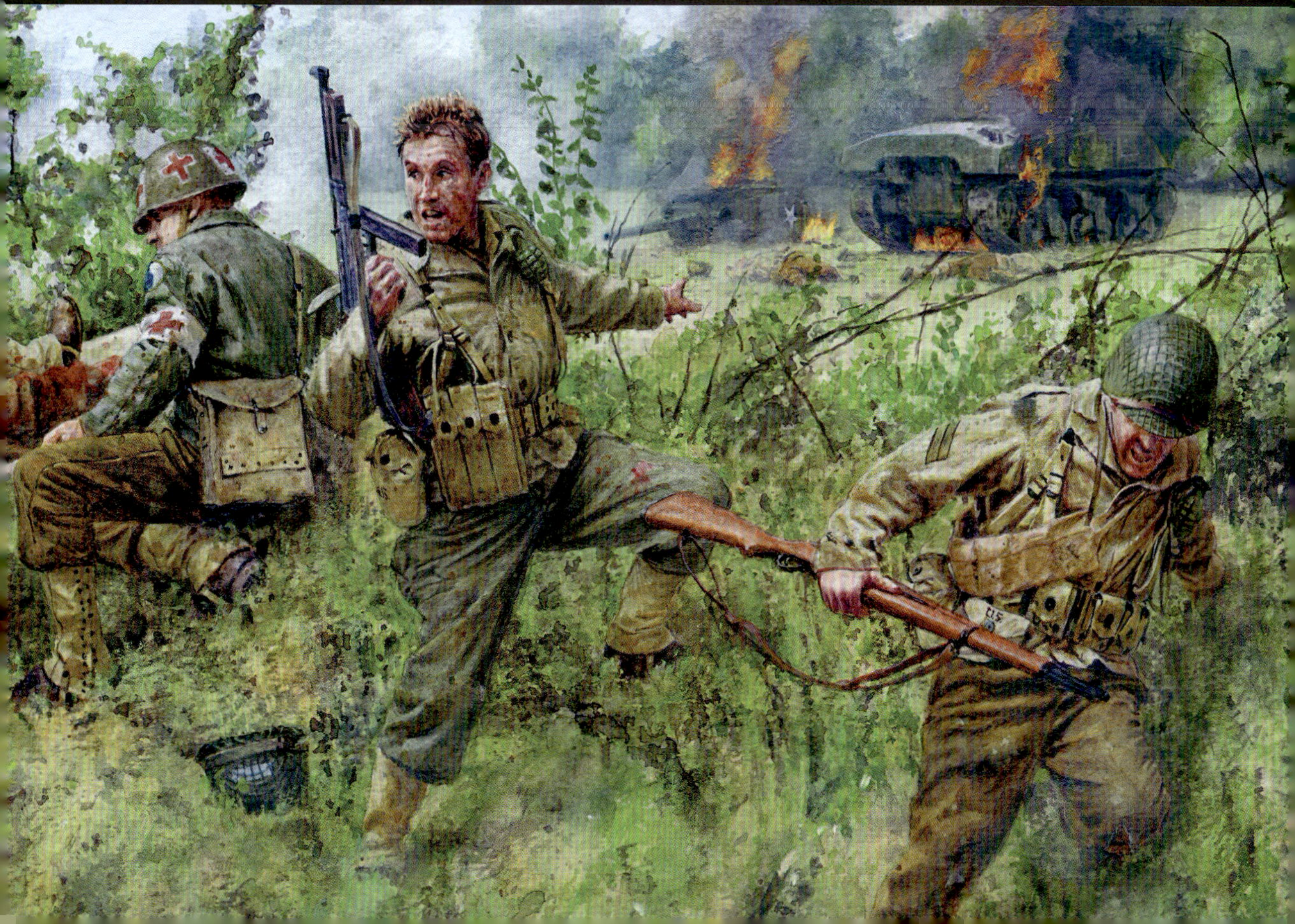

Contesting the main defensive line, July 13, 1944

German view: This shows a section of the *Hauptkampflinie* (main defensive line) held by Fallschirmjäger-Regiment 8. An earlier American attack has overrun the German outpost line, but its supporting tank has been knocked out with a *Panzerschreck* antitank rocket. A mortar-fire controller observes through binoculars, ready to call down fire on the hedgerow behind which the Americans have taken cover. An MG 42 team are ready to put down a curtain of fire while a sniper with a Gew 43 will pick off any exposed targets. While these troops are visible from this angle, the German firing positions were mostly concealed in camouflaged, deeply dug defenses protected from artillery fire.

US view: This platoon from the 175th Infantry has driven-in the German outpost line. It has been trained to use the "one squad, one tank, one field" tactics, but as the Americans attacked into the next field a mortar bomb caught the platoon commander, and the tank was knocked out. This attack has stalled. Unless something significant happens, the unit will not advance farther. Maybe a success by a flanking unit will force the Germans to withdraw or a US company or battalion commander will rustle up some artillery support and pressurize every junior leader to put themselves and their men at risk by advancing into a field covered by machine-gun and mortar fire.

Troops of the 29th Infantry Division in Saint-Lô, July 20, 1944. The first US infantry to enter the city were from the division's 1/115, commanded by Major Glover S. Johns, Jr. (US Signal Corps/Wikimedia/Public Domain)

Realizing it was a critically important moment in the battle, Gerhardt ordered all nine of his rifle battalions to take the offensive on July 17, leaving no reserves. One of these battalions, Major Thomas D. Howie's 3/116, had the most important mission of the day: to attack toward La Madeleine, join Bingham's men, and press on to Saint-Lô. With only 420 men, 3/116 was below half-strength, but it was probably the strongest rifle battalion in the 29th Infantry Division.

Howie's orders did not require 3/116 to overcome the resistance between his line of departure and Bingham's 2/116. Jumping off just before dawn, 3/116 penetrated the German lines silently and swiftly, reaching La Madeleine just as the sun was rising. Orders came over the radio ordering both battalions to move into Saint-Lô, but Howie was mortally wounded by a mortar-bomb fragment before these orders could be carried out. Both battalions were then subject to German counterattack.

On July 18, the Germans pulled back south of Saint-Lô, which fell to an armored column composed of miscellaneous units within and attached to the 29th Infantry Division and 1/115. Gerhardt ordered that Howie's body should be brought into Saint-Lô as a symbol of all the soldiers of the 29th Infantry Division who had died since D-Day (Balkoski 2005).

US soldiers crawl along a bombed-out Saint-Lô street in an effort to avoid sniper fire, July 1944. Although the Germans withdrew their defensive line south of Saint-Lô on July 18, they left snipers behind and subjected the city to a heavy bombardment, as well as penetrations by combat patrols during the night of July 18/19. (FPG/Archive Photos/Getty Images)

Mont Castré and Witches' Island

July 3–23, 1944

BACKGROUND TO BATTLE

At the close of June 1944, the First US Army was completing its first major mission ashore in Normandy: the capture of the port of Cherbourg. The next step would be to advance south through the hedgerow country. Occupying a general east–west line across the base of the Cotentin Peninsula, Major General Troy H. Middleton's VIII Corps was tasked with attacking south, three divisions (79th, 82d, and 90th) abreast, between the sea and the marshland of the Prairies Marécageuses de Gorges. Initially, VIII Corps was to seize the ground immediately north of the line Lessay–Périers. The main effort was to be made on the left, in the 90th Infantry Division's zone.

The 90th Infantry Division landed in Normandy between D-Day and D+2. Its 359th Infantry Regiment had come ashore on June 6 under command of the 4th Infantry Division. The division fought under VII Corps command during the battle for the Cotentin Peninsula. By the end of June, it had received 3,500 replacements for casualties, a new divisional commander, Major General Eugene M. Landrum, and two regimental commanders to replace officers found wanting. By June 30, the 357th Infantry was on its fourth commander, Colonel George H. Barth, while the 358th Infantry was on its second, Colonel Richard C. Partridge. Its leading role in the next operation would be a test for the new team and a challenge for unit commanders absorbing what amounted to nearly 50 percent of its establishment of infantrymen.

US intelligence assessments of German forces and their likely reactions were uncertain. There was a view that the Germans were weak and likely to withdraw if attacked, but other assessments were that the Germans would fight hard to restrict the Allies to a shallow bridgehead. American assessments of enemy strength exaggerated the fragmented nature of the survivors from the German formations engaged in the June battles for Cherbourg.

The German defenses were based on the Mahlmann Line. This had been excavated in late 1943 under the direction of Generalmajor Paul Mahlmann, the commander of the 353. Infanterie-Division, to practice the defense against an attack from the Cotentin Peninsula. Eight months later, Mahlmann's division would be defending these positions, occupying the center of the line with the remnants of the 243. Infanterie-Division to its left and the 77. Infanterie-Division to its right, with Fallschirmjäger-Regiment 15 under command. The cornerstone of the Mahlmann Line was Hill 122, which dominated observation to the north. A German observation post on Hill 122 offered views as far as Utah Beach. The German main defense line ran through Mont Castré, while there were outposts 2,190yd north. The Germans had brought up supplies of artillery ammunition and reserves, including two Panzer divisions (2. SS-Panzer-Division *Das Reich* and the Panzer-Lehr-Division), and elements of the 5. Fallschirmjäger-Division.

The LXXXIV. Armeekorps reserve was Fallschirmjäger-Regiment 15 and a *Pionier* company of the 5. Fallschirmjäger-Division. Despite the shortages of equipment and limited training within the division, Fallschirmjäger-Regiment 15 had been brought up to 95 percent of its weapon strength. Although the leadership of the 5. Fallschirmjäger-Division was subsequently criticized for the poor quality of its divisional staff, the commander of Fallschirmjäger-Regiment 15 was Major Kurt Gröschke, who had been awarded the *Ritterkreuz* for his actions in Italy preventing the Allies from breaking through at Monte Cassino in February 1944.

Prisoners of war from the 2. Fallschirmjäger-Division in the port city of Brest, guarded by soldiers from US VIII Corps, September 18, 1944. The division was not engaged in Normandy, but one of its regiments, Fallschirmjäger-Regiment 6, had been detached and operated independently. The division had also been depleted to send reinforcements to the other *Fallschirmjäger-Divisionen.* (Fred Ramage/Keystone/Hulton Archive/Getty Images)

MAP KEY

1 **July 3–5:** VIII Corps' 90th Infantry Division commences its assault on the Mahlmann Line.

2 **July 5:** The 359th Infantry assaults Point 122.

3 **July 5:** 1/358 and 2/358 assault the northeastern corner of Mont Castré.

4 **July 5–6:** 1/357 and 3/357 fight their way through Beaucoudray.

5 **July 6:** Having seized the summit of Point 122 on Mont Castré on July 5, 1/359 seizes the high ground northwest of the hamlet of La Ville, around 1,000yd southwest of Point 122.

6 **July 7–8:** Fallschirmjäger-Regiment 15 counterattacks Beaucoudray, resulting in the capture of most of two companies of 3/357.

7 **July 10:** Advancing through the forest, 3/358 fights elements of Fallschirmjäger-Regiment 15.

8 **July 11:** 1/358 and 2/358 advance east to threaten the flank of the German forces enfilading Beaucoudray.

9 **July 11:** Germans forces withdraw from the Mahlmann Line to the "Water Position" north of Périers.

10 **July 22:** 1/358 and 2/358 occupy Sèves Island.

11 **July 22:** Oberfeldwebel Uhlig's 16./FJR 6 attacks the western end of the US position on Sèves Island.

12 **July 23:** Uhlig attacks the eastern end of the American line with the support of three Panther tanks, capturing 230 prisoners. Two German machine guns cut off the US withdrawal route.

Battlefield environment

The combat discussed in this chapter took place west of the Vire River, between La Haye-du-Puits and Périers. The main conflict occurred on the eastern edge of the Mahlmann Line, a network of earthworks and field defenses between the Prairies Marécageuses de Gorges, a marsh covering nearly 4 square miles that ultimately drained into the Vire near Carentan, and the sea.

Mont Castré was an irregular hill covering some 4.6 square miles on the western half of the 90th Infantry Division's attack frontage. The feature above the 80m (262ft) contour was diamond-shaped, with a valley on the eastern side with a stream draining into the Prairies Marécageuses de Gorges. The highest points on the feature were Point 122 (meters; 400ft) on the northern tip and two spot heights, 112m (367ft) on the southern and eastern spurs. Much of the hill was covered with woods. East of the hill is a 1¼–2-mile stretch of hedgerow country between the feature and the Prairies Marécageuses de Gorges. The village of Beaucoudray sits on a spur of land between valleys draining into the Prairies Marécageuses de Gorges. The summer of 1944 was one of the wettest in living memory, with flying restricted on many days. This hampered the employment of Allied air power.

US soldiers move across a road to take cover from enemy fire in the hedgerow country near the village of Périers, July 21, 1944. Note the soldier running in the "Normandy crouch," bent over to keep his head below the hedges. (Fred Ramage/Keystone/Hulton Archive/Getty Images)

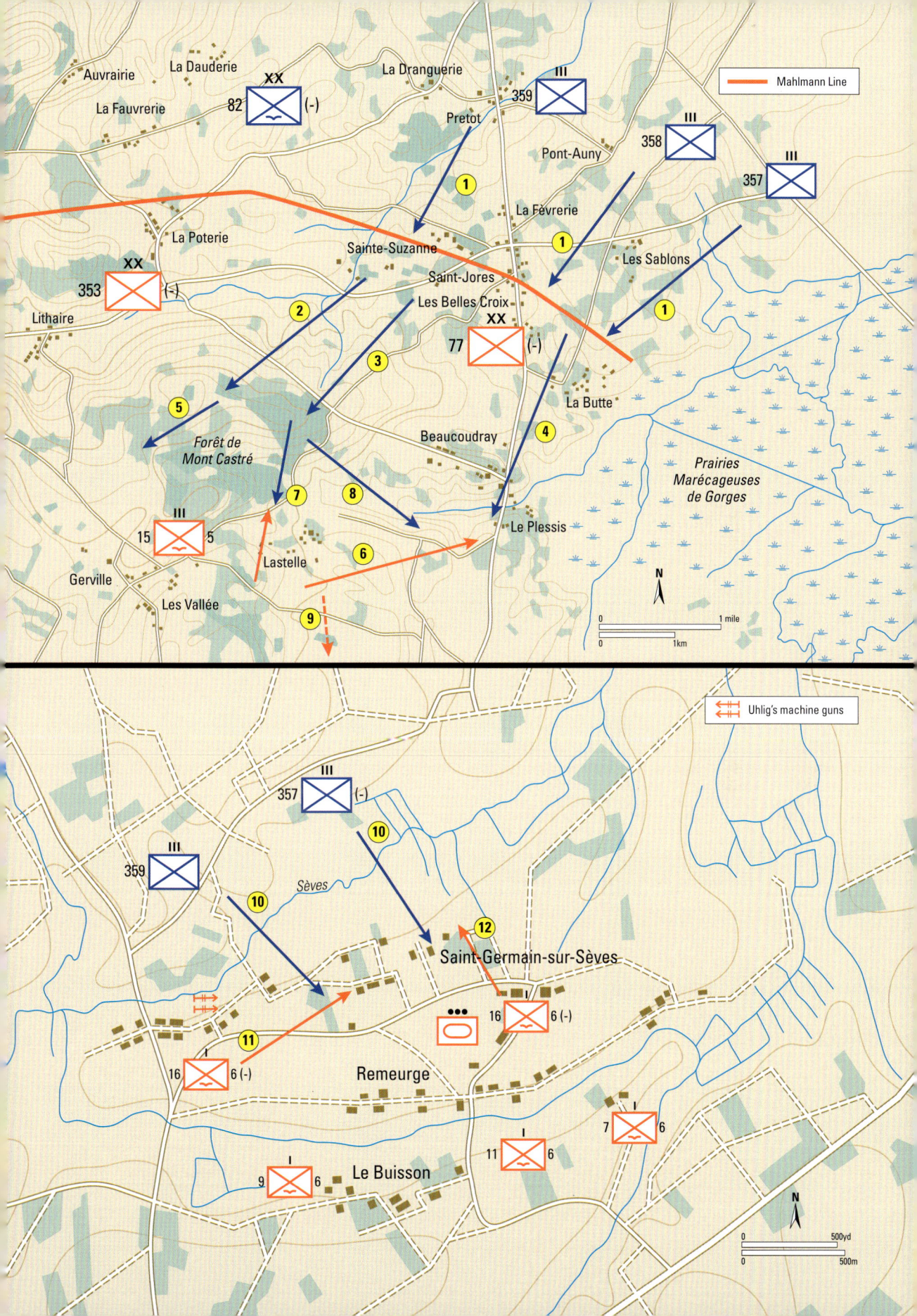

Top map labels:

Auvrairie
La Dauderie
La Drancuerie
La Fauvrerie
La Poterie
Pretot
Pont-Auny
La Fèvrerie
Sainte-Suzanne
Saint-Jores
Les Belles Croix
Les Sablons
Lithaire
La Butte
Beaucoudray
Forêt de Mont Castré
Le Plessis
Prairies Marécageuses de Gorges
Gerville
Lastelle
Les Vallée

Mahlmann Line

XX 82 (-)
III 359
III 358
III 357
XX 353 (-)
XX 77 (-)
III 15 5

1, 2, 3, 4, 5, 6, 7, 8, 9

N

0 — 1 mile
0 — 1km

Bottom map labels:

Uhlig's machine guns

III 357 (-)
III 359
Sèves
Saint-Germain-sur-Sèves
Remeurge
Le Buisson

I 16 6 (-)
I 16 6 (-)
I 11 6
I 7 6
I 9 6

10, 10, 11, 12

N

0 — 500yd
0 — 500m

INTO COMBAT

Major General Landrum's plan was a simultaneous assault by the 358th Infantry Regiment and 359th Infantry Regiment, with the 358th Infantry seeking to outflank the Mont Castré feature from the east while the 359th Infantry conducted a frontal attack from the north. The 357th Infantry would be committed through the eastern corridor toward the objective area beyond the hill. The 90th Infantry Division would be supported by the 712th Tank and 606th Tank Destroyer battalions. Artillery support would include the division's organic four howitzer battalions, a battalion of the corps artillery, and the artillery of the 4th Infantry Division.

The assault was launched at 0530hrs on July 3, preceded by a 15-minute artillery bombardment. Heavy rain prevented Allied fighter-bombers and observation aircraft from taking off. The next three days were a pattern of assaults launched around 0600hrs, making around 1–2 miles per day but at heavy cost against the German outpost line manned by Heer units. By the end of July 5, 1/357 with armor from the 712th Tank Battalion advanced south from Saint-Jores to Beaucoudray. The same day the 359th Infantry set out to assault Point 122 on Mont Castré with 2/359 on the left and 3/359 on the right. By the end of the day, the Americans had advanced 2,000yd and had a foothold on the Mont Castré feature, albeit at a heavy cost. While 2/359 had seized the high ground on the north side of the woods, 3/359 was checked short of its objectives, on the slopes of the feature.

On July 6 the 90th Infantry Division continued its attacks. On the left, 3/357 attacked south of the stream running through Beaucoudray, with 1/357 following up. By evening, after bitter fighting, the companies of 1/357 and 3/357 occupied a narrow salient south of Beaucoudray. Until now, the 90th Infantry Division had faced Heer troops. Shortly before midnight, however, Fallschirmjäger-Regiment 15 launched a violent counterattack against the three companies (Co. I, Co. L, and Co. C) south of Beaucoudray. Co. C was forced back with heavy casualties, and intermingled with Co. K. These two depleted companies subsequently fought as one company for the next several days. Co. I and Co. L held firm, but were soon cut off from the remainder of the 357th Infantry by German infiltration. This was the start of 36 hours of German counterattacks against the overextended 357th Infantry, with support from German armor, probably the assault guns of Fallschirm-Sturmgeschütz-Brigade 12:

> Cooks, drivers, antitank and service personnel were organized into a provisional company and put into the line to plug up gaps between the seriously depleted battalions. By dark on the 7th, the combined remnants of companies "C" and "K" had repulsed fourteen counterattacks supported by tanks. Hand-to-hand fighting was raging in the "I" and "L" Company areas. These companies were surrounded and cut off from the rear and were being attacked from all sides. Lack of ammunition finally forced the surrender of the major part of these units. (Roeder 1945)

On July 6, 1/359 seized the high ground northwest of the hamlet of La Ville around 1,000yd southwest of Point 122. To 1/359's left (east), 3/359 met

This sharp-toothed hedgerow plow, improvised by the Allies from captured German beach obstacles, was used to clear paths through the famed Normandy hedgerows from mid-July 1944. It is a more sophisticated version of the two steel prongs welded on the front of tanks of the 741st and 747th Tank battalions that supported the 2d and 29th Infantry divisions. This is an M5 light tank, with sandbags liberally applied to the front hull to try to improve the vehicle's frontal protection. (© CORBIS/Corbis via Getty Images)

heavy resistance in the thick woods on the summit and became embroiled in a close-quarter grenade and bayonet melee, which continued until mid-afternoon when the German resistance was broken. At this point 3/359 was able to push to its objective east of 1/359. Before it could organize itself, 3/359 received a vigorous counterattack and repulsed it with difficulty. At the end of the day, the two US battalions were isolated with a sizable German force between them. Small groups of German troops were behind them, and resupply was only possible on the backs of tanks that crashed trails through the brush.

Meanwhile, on the northeastern side of Mont Castré, 2/359 and 1/358, under command of the 359th Infantry, assaulted the eastern nose of the feature at 0830hrs, taking their objectives with little resistance. This position offered a commanding view north and east. German prisoners captured in the morning were *Fallschirmjäger*.

The 358th Infantry, with two remaining battalions, was tasked with clearing the area north of the 359th Infantry. The entire front was alive throughout the night. Shortly after midnight a *Fallschirmjäger* battalion scaled the wooded south slopes of the nose occupied by 1/358 and launched a noisily fanatical assault which retook the high ground, driving the Americans back onto the reverse (northern) slope. *Fallschirmjäger* elements infiltrated down into the valley. The Germans between 1/359 and 3/359 were active and small-scale attacks against 3/359 continued from the east and south. German mortar and artillery fell everywhere on the 90th Infantry Division front.

On the morning of July 7, 2/358 passed under command of the 359th Infantry for deployment between the division's isolated 1/359 and 2/359, fighting forward and clearing resistance between the battalions by 2250hrs, while 2/359 and 1/358 on the eastern side of the feature came under command of the 358th Infantry on the northeastern corner of Mont Castré, where 1/358 fought a seesaw battle on the crest to reduce the German penetration that threatened the right flank of the 357th Infantry. On the western side of the feature, the 359th Infantry broke up a series of attacks from the west using divisional and corps artillery.

On the morning of July 8, the situation looked unpromising for the 90th Infantry Division. The planned deployment of the 8th Infantry Division into the western section of the divisional area was delayed. Worse still was the situation of the 357th Infantry. A counterattack by Co. E to relieve the regiment's isolated companies, Co. I and Co. L, did not take place due to a "failure to organize it properly" (Roeder 1945). The CO of 3/357 was relieved of his command and the remnants of his battalion were placed under command of 1/357. A few men of Co. I and Co. L trickled back later in the day. There were no sounds of battle from their last reported positions. The 357th Infantry's regimental train and headquarters were formed into a provisional company and placed astride the Saint-Jores–Beaucoudray road to prevent any German exploitation of their success. German pressure slackened, however, and it became apparent that the *Fallschirmjäger* had been withdrawn and replaced with "less elite" troops (Roeder 1945).

July 9 seems to have been a day of consolidation for the 357th Infantry and 358th Infantry, while the 359th Infantry contained continuous probing and attacks. On July 10, in response to dubious intelligence from VIII Corps that the Germans had begun a general withdrawal, the 357th Infantry was ordered to send out strong patrols to determine the presence or absence of the enemy. These patrols were met with heavy fire that indicated the Germans were very much still there, established in emplacements with overhead cover and immune to artillery fire.

What should have been a coordinated advance by the 358th Infantry and 359th Infantry on July 10 was replaced with an advance by the 358th Infantry only, with the 359th Infantry to advance on their right as soon as practical. At 1400hrs, 3/358 attacked southeast into the reverse slope of the woods, with a strength in its rifle companies of 434 men and 13 officers. The ground was rocky and densely wooded. Control was "difficult" (Roeder 1945). The only route through the attack area was a firebreak, on which Co. L, the left-hand assault company, advanced. Despite severe resistance, 3/358 initially made good progress and halted on its first phase line to restore lateral control, and with the aid of colored-smoke shells, a check on their own location. Almost immediately after resuming the advance, 3/358's assault platoons ran into fierce resistance from the *Fallschirmjäger*, with the Germans using grenades and machine guns from trees, spider holes, and carefully concealed dug-in positions in the tangled undergrowth. The action was resolved by the "gallant action of those men not pinned to the ground, who charged the Germans with bayonet, grenades and hip fired machine guns" (Roeder 1945).

The battalion command group was attacked by a bypassed German squad. According to the Distinguished Service Cross citation for Lieutenant Colonel Jacob W. Bealke, Jr., CO 3/358:

Approximately 20 paratroopers from the elite 5th German Parachute Division, attacked fanatically, screaming, throwing hand grenades and firing machine pistols. Colonel Bealke, killed two of the enemy with hand grenades, wounded a third and took two others prisoner. The enemy formation broke. A second German group

Oberstleutnant Friedrich August Freiherr von der Heydte, commander of Fallschirmjäger-Regiment 6, in conversation with SS-Brigadeführer Werner von Ostendorf, commander of the 17. SS-Panzergrenadier-Division *Götz von Berlichingen*, near Carentan in mid-June 1944. Heydte would emerge from the war with a reputation for chivalry. The US official history records how he sent back US medical staff taken prisoner with the message that the Americans needed them more than he did. (ullstein bild/ullstein bild via Getty Images)

then attacked from the right flank, but Colonel Bealke killed two with his pistol, one falling at his feet. Twenty additional soldiers arrived (from Company L) as reinforcement just before a third enemy group attacked from the rear of Colonel Bealke's group. Of the 3rd attacking party 3 were killed, 8 taken prisoner and the remainder disappeared.

While Bealke's battalion halted for reorganization, a gap emerged between the leading companies as Co. I diverged to storm a German platoon position on a rocky knoll on its northeastern flank, which had been inflicting heavy casualties. In the words of his Distinguished Service Cross citation, PFC Theodore G. Wagner,

> on his own initiative, worked his way forward scaling a 25-foot rocky hill, in order to reach the enemy strong point from which the fire was coming. At great risk he attained his objective and silenced the enemy guns by throwing several hand grenades into the position. He then forced eight enemy soldiers to surrender to him; nine others were found dead behind the hill.

The original assault companies, Co. L and Co. I, were placed on the flanks while Co. K assaulted through the gap with the support of M4 tanks from 1st Platoon, Co. C, 712th Tank Battalion. Co. K broke out of the woods and reached a position overlooking Lastelle, 3/358's objective. Four of the tanks were knocked out by antitank guns and handheld weapons. After suffering a heavy, persistent bombardment, Co. K withdrew to form the front of the battalion perimeter. By the end of the first day Bealke and 11 of the 17 officers were casualties, but 3/358 was within 75yd of the initial objective. The units to the right (west) of 3/358 were held up. This was the decisive act in the battle for Mont Castré (Bryan 1945).

On July 11, 1/358 and 2/358 swept the eastern half of the woods and 2/359, still under command, advanced east to enfilade the resistance to the

Pictured following the award of his *Ritterkreuz*, Oberfeldwebel Alexander Uhlig was a company commander in Fallschirmjäger-Regiment 6. He was awarded the *Ritterkreuz* in recognition of his participation in the July 23 early-morning counterattack on 1/358 (90th Infantry Division). Uhlig was captured by US forces near Saint-Michel at the end of July 1944 and sent to a prisoner-of-war camp in England and later to Missouri, USA, before escaping from captivity in April 1947 and returning to Leipzig, his home town. (MYCHELE DANIAU/AFP via Getty Images)

357th Infantry. Conducted on a narrow front and flanked on both sides, the advance ran into heavy resistance and halted by 1500hrs. Meanwhile, the 359th Infantry, with 2/357 under command, swung left and advanced southeast toward Lastelle in an attack coordinated with 3/358. By this time, 3/358 was composed of the remnants of the three rifle companies, reorganized into one composite company with a strength of 126 men and commanded by a lieutenant. The composite company advanced east during the mid-afternoon to the road north of Lastelle before attacking south. In a renewed charge, the depleted 3/358 overran the objective, killed 40 enemy, and captured eight machine guns, antitank rocket launchers, and mortars. Lastelle fell to the Americans around midnight. In the early hours of July 12 the Germans pulled back from the Mahlmann Line to new positions 3,280yd farther south. The battle for Mont Castré was over.

According to the after-action report, the 90th Infantry Division's commanders considered that they had done well: "Blood, guts and superior equipment had finally broken the Mahlman [*sic*] Line … The 90th Div, drained as it was of key officers and non-commissioned officers had undisputedly proven its combat effectiveness. For 9 continuous days and nights it had fought without respite against a seasoned and entrenched enemy, and its wounds notwithstanding, emerged from the fight victorious and high-spirited."

The action of 3/358 on July 10 had been decisive in breaking the German resistance and was recognized later in the year by the award of a Presidential Unit Citation for the Mahlmann Line action, and the Distinguished Service Cross for its commander, Lieutenant Colonel Bealke. The cost was very high on both sides, however. The 90th Infantry Division suffered 5,000 casualties, killed, wounded, and taken prisoner. Around 80 percent of these would have been from the 5,000–6,000 men in the rifle companies. For the *Fallschirmjäger*, the cost was also very high. From June 15, when the first elements of Fallschirmjäger-Regiment 15 began operations, through July 10, losses amounted to 70 percent of their strength in terms of men killed or wounded.

William E. DePuy

Born in Jamestown, North Dakota, on October 1, 1919, William Eugene DePuy joined the South Dakota National Guard as a teenager; he graduated from South Dakota State University in 1941 and received a Reserve Officers' Training Corps (ROTC) commission. His first assignment was as a platoon commander with the 20th Infantry Regiment. During his time as a platoon leader, his platoon marched 500 miles to and from the Louisiana maneuvers. He joined the 357th Infantry Regiment (90th Infantry Division) in 1942 as the S3 (operations and training officer) of 1/357 and then became the regimental S3.

By the end of World War II, DePuy had been awarded the Distinguished Service Cross, three Silver Stars, and two Purple Hearts. He ended the war as a 25-year-old battalion commander with a reputation for showing intelligence and initiative on the battlefield, notably during nighttime infiltration attacks; he was also keen to minimize casualties among his men. Drawing upon his formative experiences as a soldier with the 357th Infantry in Normandy, DePuy was a stern critic of what he saw in the preparations for D-Day, noting an absence of tactical training and an over-reliance on completing the plan rather than assessing combat performance. In particular, he highlighted the failure to prepare for poor visibility in Normandy and its effects on firepower and command and control. Damning of the performance of the 357th Infantry's initial commander, DePuy praised Colonel George H. Barth, who assumed command on June 16, 1944, and transformed the fortunes of his regiment, restoring its morale and effectiveness despite severe casualties.

After 1945 DePuy became a regular officer serving in diplomatic and staff roles and field commands in Europe and Vietnam, where he commanded the 1st Infantry Division. In 1977 he was appointed the first commander of the US Army Training and Doctrine Command (TRADOC), in which role he created the mechanisms to restore the US Army's self-image as a conventional combat force trained and configured for continental warfare. William DePuy retired from active duty in 1977 and died on September 9, 1992.

The 90th Infantry Division followed the withdrawing Germans to the line of the Sèves River, with the 357th Infantry and 358th Infantry overlooking the island between two waterways, known as the "Island of the White Witches," about 1 mile northeast of Périers (Anon 1945: 11). During July 16–21, depleted rifle companies were augmented with replacements. The next task was to force a passage across the island and hold it to provide the division with a better line of departure for Operation *Cobra*. The approaches to the island were devoid of cover and swept by German fire. On July 21, 1/358 and 2/358 attacked

> against overwhelming odds, gaining a foothold on the island, only to be severely counterattacked, with the enemy throwing in everything he had in an all-out effort to retain control of his main line of resistance. Eventually, after butting against impregnable enemy defenses and being subjected to unusually large concentrations of enemy artillery and tank fire, the attack was repulsed amid heavy losses. (Anon 1945: 11)

The German version of events is slightly different. At 0600hrs on July 22, a bombardment commenced on the positions of 11./FJR 6, which was defending the area north of Saint-Germain-sur-Sèves. The Americans managed to push back the company's forward-deployed elements and built a bridgehead at the crossing.

Major von der Heydte, Fallschirmjäger-Regiment 6's commander, realized that the American advance had to be stopped. Because of the high losses in the past weeks, the only part of the regiment that was available for this responsibility was 16./FJR 6 with five NCOs and 27 *Jäger* under the leadership of Oberfeldwebel Alexander Uhlig. His mission was to push the Americans back over the Sèves, in order to restore the former main line of resistance. Uhlig was given complete freedom of action and the right to subordinate soldiers from other companies. Whenever possible he was to capture two or three prisoners. Uhlig and his men set off armed with rifles, pistols, submachine guns, hand grenades, and rifle grenades, toward an 875yd-wide area occupied by the Americans. Aware that he faced more than 300 US troops, Uhlig resolved to attack the American right flank near Sèves, where the GIs were the most thinly spread.

Stealthily making their way toward Sèves without being detected, the *Fallschirmjäger* reached their objective and commenced their flank attack at about 1800hrs, the unexpected direction of the German assault taking the Americans by surprise. During the ensuing three hours, the GIs were pushed back about 385yd. Uhlig noted that 16./FJR 6 lost no men during the action (Griesser 2011). At the end of the day Uhlig's company had four NCOs and 24 enlisted men on their feet. Hearing the Americans digging in against an attack from this quarter, he decided to mount a second attack from the opposite, eastern flank. He sought and obtained reinforcements – a platoon of three Panther medium tanks, and an NCO and 15 soldiers new to the front and armed with two MG 42s. Uhlig decided that the newly arrived troops would be a liability in the attack and deployed them to cover the approaches to the bridge, with orders to shoot at Americans attacking or retreating. Concerned about the threat posed by handheld antitank weapons, he decided that the *Fallschirmjäger* would lead with the Panthers following.

July 27, 1944: soldiers from the 359th Infantry Regiment (90th Infantry Division) advance amid bomb- and shell-damaged buildings toward the church of Saint-Pierre-et-Saint-Paul on the Rue de Carentan in Périers. The photograph was taken a few days after the debacle on Sèves Island. (Hugh Broderick/Pool/Keystone/Hulton Archive/Getty Images)

Shortly before 0800hrs the Panthers deployed and the attack started with the *Fallschirmjäger* firing their weapons. The firefight began. The American response was a heavy artillery barrage, which was brought closer: "We were forced to attack, so to speak. During the pandemonium, our opponents disappeared into their foxholes. Because of this we could storm forward and so escape the artillery fire. One of the tanks broke down, and the second became wedged in a collapsed building." The Americans had not realized how few Germans were attacking and some started to surrender. Others started to withdraw toward the bridge, at which point the German machine guns opened fire. By 1100hrs the battle was over and Uhlig's men had captured 234 prisoners, including 11 officers, including both battalion commanders (Griesser 2011: 134). This was arguably the last successful action conducted by the 7. Armee in Normandy and was recognized by the award of the *Ritterkreuz* to Uhlig.

Analysis

The battles among the hedgerows of Normandy were not decided by superior artillery. In the Saint-Lô sector, it was ultimately a conflict at close range between US infantrymen and *Fallschirmjäger* fighting over individual hedgerows and fields. The US soldiers eventually prevailed in the battles for Saint-Lô, though they endured many setbacks and suffered high casualties. Despite the disparity in numbers, the *Fallschirmjäger* resisted for much longer than the Allies expected and emerged with an enhanced reputation for determination and aggression.

Fallschirmjäger casualties in Normandy, probably Fallschirmjäger-Regiment 6's dead in the Carentan area, killed in the fighting against US airborne troops. (Galerie Bilderwelt/Getty Images)

TERRAIN

The starting point is the extent to which the *bocage* affected the combatants' experience. Hedgerows were a surprise to all of the US troops. Like most armies, the US Army's tactical manuals were based on open terrain with rolling hills, a few small woods, and villages. There were chapters covering warfare in the "special conditions" of mountains, woods, and towns, but there was no section covering hedgerow terrain. Yet the hedgerow countryside had many of the features of fighting in woods: forested land with lots of regular clearings; short engagement ranges; and vegetation that provided cover for movement and observation. The German *Truppenführung* was no more help. By 1944, however, the Germans had spent three years of fighting in the Soviet Union, where the landscape of the northern half of the country was largely forest and swamp. The German tactical notes about the special conditions of fighting in Russian swamps and woods are revealing:

> In forest fighting, commanders can easily lose control of their troops … Limited observation, the intensified noise of combat, and the excitement created by fighting at close quarters make it difficult to distinguish between friend and foe, increase the danger of overestimating purely local events, and the danger of panic is thereby aggravated … Here the individual fighting man assumes even greater importance than during combat in open terrain. Fighting at close quarters plays a major role and numerical superiority is less significant than personal courage. Light and heavy infantry weapons, submachine guns, machine pistols, hand grenades, bayonets, the long hunting knife, and flame throwers are the most suitable weapons for this type of combat … Radio communications are particularly important. Mapping may be unreliable, and aircraft are important for reconnaissance. (Department of the Army 1951: 5–10)

Major Thomas H Howie's body was ceremonially brought to Saint-Lô on a Jeep with 3/116. Howie had commanded this battalion for four days during the critical stage of the attack on Saint-Lô, before his fatal wound on July 16. The divisional commander had given Howie a verbal order to enter Saint-Lô and decided that the ceremonial arrival of Howie would represent the sacrifices of all of the division's casualties. This image was widely circulated in the media as that of "the Major of Saint-Lô." (Associated Press/Alamy Stock Photo)

TECHNOLOGY AND ORGANIZATION

The Germans entered hedgerow combat with better-suited weapons than the US infantry. The Americans had a major advantage in the weight of indirect fire from infantry and chemical mortars, and field artillery. In hedgerow fighting, however, it was difficult to bring large-caliber weapons to bear at close ranges. The US Army infantry squad, platoon, and company did not carry enough handheld weapons to win the firefight against comparable *Fallschirmjäger* units. US soldiers perceived that their firearms generated significantly more smoke than German weapons, which was a disincentive against speculative fire, and lowered levels of participation in firefights. It was difficult to deploy the tripod-mounted machine guns that equipped heavy-weapons companies and platoons, thus depriving the infantry of much of their firepower. These were problems that were evident by mid-June 1944.

As can be seen in the text, the 2d Infantry Division took measures at various levels to improve firepower. Swapping 100 M1 carbines for Thompson submachine guns from supply and antiaircraft artillery units doubled the number of automatic weapons in each squad in 1/23. Improvised pintle mounts enabled .30-caliber M1919 Browning light machine guns to be deployed forward with rifle squads. Stripping .50-caliber M2 Browning heavy machine guns from the antiaircraft mounts in vehicles allowed the creation of extra HMG elements manned by drivers and clerks. Adding telephones to tanks, conducting training in tank–infantry cooperation, and providing a tank per assault squad gave a massive increment to the US troops' firepower.

Low-level tactics were rarely employed according to the diagrams in the tactical manuals. For the individual soldier the orders would be some variant of "capture the next hedge," "shoot at anyone in your arc of fire," or "follow me as we sneak along this hedgerow." Tactically, the Germans were better prepared for fighting in the hedgerows. The initial mission of II. Fallschirmkorps was as an antiairborne force. Their training was based on small units and guerrilla warfare. The emphasis on swift actions and counterattacks by junior commanders and individuals was suited to the hedgerow fighting in June and July. As shown by the Germans' June 11 attack on 1/115, infantry attacks closely followed artillery and mortar barrages. In all three of the actions by different US infantry divisions, the preference throughout June and July was for frontal assaults. To a certain extent, this was a consequence of what historian Russell F. Weigley (1960) refers to as "The American Way of War," i.e. a preference for overwhelming an enemy with the constant pressure of attacks on a broad front relying on the mass of manpower and materiel that could be replaced by US institutions and industry.

US troops learned quickly, but needed a quiet period to develop new procedures. This was granted to the 2d and 29th Infantry divisions in the three-week lull at the end of June. The unlucky 90th Infantry Division went from initial costly and unhappy experiences in the Cotentin to Mont Castré and Sèves island. During this period, the 90th Infantry Division was losing around 45 percent of its platoon commanders each week and each phase of fighting was undertaken with replacements making up around half the manpower in rifle companies. Major Henry G. Spencer, who commanded 1/23 in June 1944, tried to persuade his divisional commander, Major General

US troops in Saint-Lô following its capture, July 18 1944. If this photograph has been captioned correctly, these must be some of the troops of Task Force C, or 1/115, which had been reduced to a couple of hundred riflemen. The devastation caused by Allied bombing and shelling by both sides gives a good idea of what "Liberation" meant for many towns and villages in Normandy. (Glasshouse Vintage/Universal History Archive/Universal Images Group via Getty Images)

Walter M. Robertson, to conduct a night attack on Hill 192, infiltrating the thin line of defenders. Robertson turned down the idea because he did not think the troops could carry out the maneuver. After the heavy fighting in Normandy was over the 90th Infantry Division adopted many tactical adaptations, including a preference for nighttime infiltration to seize vital ground, and an emphasis on firepower to attrite the inevitable counterattacks.

In his postwar report on the July 11 battle, Lieutenant Colonel Frank T. Mildren, the commander of 1/38, considered that the tendency to make detailed plans detracted from flexibility: "We had included plans even for rifle squads, and when those squads suffered heavy casualties --we had lost 194 men in this attack --then the plan disintegrated. This lack of flexibility was probably induced by my overconfidence. I thought with all the fire support I had that the attack would be an easy advance" (Mildren 1947: 11). William DePuy, in July 1944 the 357th Infantry's operations officer, reflected later that the German tactics avoided frontal attacks. The 14 German attacks on the 357th Infantry reported in the fighting for Beaucoudray during July 7–8 were supported by a couple of assault guns. The Germans probed for weakness, then used fire and maneuver to overcome the US company positions (Brownlee & Mullen 2015: 38–39).

Uhlig's decision to avoid frontal attacks given the imbalance in troop numbers is a clue to the pattern of the *Fallschirmjäger*'s response to American attacks. The *Fallschirmjäger* invariably sought to find a flank or a gap. There seem to have been few of what the Germans describe as *Gegenangriffe* (counterattacks), that is to say formal attacks organized by a higher command, probably because there were few reserves available. When the Germans did launch a counterattack the result was often a bloody repulse, as against 2/358 on Mont Castré, against 1/115 on July 11, and against 1/116 on July 15.

LEADERSHIP

Not all of the American adaptations were to tackle the specific problems associated with hedgerow fighting. Accounts from each of the US infantry divisions include painful examples of the need for time-honored combat drills such as mounting sentries and outposts, and enforcing a "stand to arms" order at dawn and dusk. Armies are bureaucracies that accrue reams of regulations, mainly concerning minor points. These regulations are often regarded as burdensome. Separating the vital from the trivial took a little while. The troops of the 29th Infantry Division would have probably been better served if Major General Gerhardt had focused more on battlefield discipline than litter, muddy vehicles, and tight helmet chinstraps.

Shortfalls in battle discipline and tactics are a function of leadership, and this was the first experience of green US troops. No amount of training could compensate for the lack of battle experience. One key difference between US troops and the *Fallschirmjäger* was the experience of the commanders at all levels.

The fighting all depended on the relatively small numbers of active fighters – the "Gutful Men" of the British tactical theorist Lionel Wigram or the 10–15 percent of participants noted by American military historian and theorist S.L.A. Marshall. Even more important was for NCOs and officers to show courage and inspire frightened men who might otherwise allow fear and lethargy to erode their offensive capabilities. The history of each of the US infantry formations is full of accounts of the pressure downward, from division through intermediate commands to squads, to get troops to move forward. Engagements weeded out those men unsuited for combat, crucially in command positions at every level, from company to divisional commanders.

Furthermore, fatigue had an impact. American accounts tell of units attacking day after day, pressured down the chain of command, but the reality may have been closer to DePuy's recollections of his own experience; noting that after several days of combat his regiment became unable to mount offensive action, its disorganization and low morale meaning that orders to attack came to nothing (Brownlee & Mullen 2015: 38).

The US experience contrasts with the action by Uhlig and his platoon-sized company from 16./FJR 6. He appears to have been given wide latitude about how he performed his mission and seems to have been under less time pressure than American company commanders. As an NCO, Uhlig wielded the authority of his regimental commander to marshal tanks and men for his mission. This is an example of the *Auftragstaktik* ("mission command") approach that postwar Western armies attempted to copy.

General der Fallschirmtruppe Eugen Meindl presents *Fallschirmjäger* with the *Ritterkreuz*, June 21, 1944. Despite their recent formation, the *Fallschirmjäger* performed remarkably well, though we do not know to what extent the Germans had problems of nonparticipation in combat. It may or may not have been harder to "shirk" combat in the *Fallschirmjäger*. Did faith in the Führer and the final Axis victory stiffen the resolve of the German airborne troops waiting in their foxholes to be overrun by the "Amies?" (Bundesarchiv, Bild_101I-585-2187-26/ Wikimedia/CC-BY-SA 3.0 DE)

Aftermath

With the capture of Saint-Lô, the First US Army had secured the start line for the breakout from the Normandy beachhead. This was initiated with Operation *Cobra*, which was supported by a massive aerial bombardment. The US Army's VII Corps overran the weakened German defenses, eroded by the heavy casualties sustained in the hedgerow fighting. This did not end the fighting, however. The 29th Infantry Division had a particularly tough fight for Vire, while the 90th Infantry Division played a significant role in

"Hun Chaser," an M4A4 medium tank in the HQ Company of the 747th Tank Battalion, supporting the 29th Infantry Division, on the rubble-strewn Rue du Neufbourg in Saint-Lô. Colt M1911 pistol in hand, a tanker surveys the terrain through his binoculars. (US Signal Corps/Public Domain)

US soldiers of the 35th Infantry Division on patrol in Saint-Lô, July 1944. The division's 134th Infantry took over from 1/115 in Saint-Lô at 0440hrs on July 19. (© Hulton-Deutsch Collection/CORBIS/Corbis via Getty Images)

closing the Falaise Pocket in late August. All three of the US infantry divisions had learned from their experience in Normandy and ended the war as veteran formations. The 90th Infantry Division was one of the key elements of the Third US Army while the 2d Infantry Division had a particularly distinguished record in the Ardennes. The 29th Infantry Division suffered 20,000 battle casualties in the 11 months from June 6, by which time only a handful of men remained from those who landed on D-Day.

The troops of the 3. Fallschirmjäger-Division fought their way out of the Falaise Pocket, but the division was overrun and destroyed in the Mons Pocket in early September. The division was re-formed in the fall of 1944, but its performance in the Ardennes did not match its former record of tactical knowhow and tenacity. Also rebuilt after Normandy, the 5 Fallschirmjäger-Division performed creditably in the Ardennes, delaying Patton's relief of Bastogne.

September 1944: a *Fallschirmjäger* who took the advice of an Allied leaflet and surrendered to US troops in France has handed over his surrender pass, guaranteeing him safe passage, to a US Army lieutenant. By the middle of September 1944, most of the personnel of the 3. and 5. Fallschirmjäger-Divisionen were prisoners, in hospital, or dead. By September 4, the 3. Fallschirmjäger-Division listed 16,370 men as missing. Allied intelligence noted that most the *Fallschirmjäger* prisoners still claimed that Germany would win the war. (Photo12/UIG/Getty Images)

Generalleutnant Schimpf, badly wounded in the breakout from the Falaise Pocket, was awarded the *Ritterkreuz* in October 1944 and the *Deutsches Kreuz in Gold* in January 1945 in recognition of his leadership in Normandy. After the war he joined the new Luftwaffe in 1957 and retired as a *Generalmajor* in 1961. Major von der Heydte led the German parachute drop in the Ardennes where he was captured. After the war he combined an academic career as a professor of international law with service in the Bundeswehr, retiring as a *Brigadegeneral der Reserve*.

Major General Gerhardt commanded the 29th Infantry Division for the rest of the war. He subsequently became subject to criticism concerning his style of leadership, and was blamed for the division's high number of casualties and for lapses in morality, having organized a brothel for the division called the Blue and Grey Riding School. He was demoted to colonel, but retired as a major general. Lieutenant Colonel Johns served as commander of 1/115 for the rest of the war. He would later command the 1st Battle Group, 18th Infantry Regiment, 8th Infantry Division that drove to Berlin from West Germany as a show of force during the Berlin Wall crisis of 1961.

The wartime reputations of the forces and personalities have remained the subject of analysis and debate. US military schools studied the actions in the hedgerows at length, and their reports form some of the reference sources for this work. The fighting in Normandy also prompted a degree of introspection within the US Army. Besides the deficiencies of the replacement system and the nature of battle shock, it also raised questions about what has been described as "The American Way of War."

UNIT ORGANIZATIONS

Fallschirmjäger-Bataillon

Like the US Army infantry battalion, each German *Fallschirmjäger-Bataillon* was part of a regiment. Each battalion (I–III) consisted of three rifle companies (numbered 1–3 in the first battalion, 5–7 in the second, and 9–11 in the third) and one heavy-weapons company (4, 8, and 12). Nominally commanded by a *Hauptmann* (captain), companies were often led by a *Leutnant* or even a senior NCO.

Each rifle company, with a notional strength of 170, had a 35-man headquarters, including an NCO and four messengers, an eight-man section with four handheld antitank weapons, and a 22-man troop with three 8cm mortars; three *Züge* (platoons), each with a headquarters group and three *Gruppen* (sections); and the *Tross* (train), 17 men led by a *Hauptfeldwebel* (equivalent to a first sergeant or company sergeant major), which provided the company's logistical support, including its cooks.

The platoon headquarters group included a platoon leader – either a junior office or a senior NCO – plus an NCO, an armorer, and four messengers. Each ten-man *Gruppe*, led by a group leader and his assistant, was armed with one or two 7.92mm MG 34 or MG 42 light machine guns, two submachine guns, and four rifles, one with a telescopic sight. The weapons in the *Gruppe* could be supplemented with the 7.92mm FG 42 select-fire automatic rifle and/or the 7.92mm Gew 43 semiautomatic rifle. In theory the platoon was transported in two 3-ton trucks, but motor transport was mostly absent from II. Fallschirmkorps.

Each heavy-weapons company was armed with 12 8cm mortars and eight tripod-mounted MG 34s or MG 42s, plus two howitzers. The regiment had three additional subunits that could support a battalion: a heavy-mortar company numbered 13, with nine 12cm mortars and eight machine guns; an antitank company numbered 14, with four 7.5cm antitank guns, 34 *Panzerschreck* rocket launchers, and six machine guns; and a *Pionier* (combat engineer) company numbered 15, with two 8cm mortars and six machine guns, two of them tripod-mounted. There was also a reconnaissance platoon, which was expanded in Fallschirmjäger-Regiment 6 to become the 16th company. These theoretical establishments varied in practice.

US infantry battalion

In July 1944, a US Army infantry battalion was composed of a headquarters company, three rifle companies, and a heavy-weapons company. Each company bore a letter designation, with A–D in the first ("Red") battalion, E–H in the second ("White"), and I–M in the third ("Blue"). There was never a Co. J.

On paper, a rifle company included six officers and 186 enlisted men. It was led, in theory, by a captain, assisted by an executive officer, though often the company commander might be a lieutenant. Each rifle company was divided into three rifle platoons and one weapons platoon, each commanded by a lieutenant. Each rifle platoon was made up of three rifle squads. The weapons platoon included two light-machine-gun squads and three 60mm mortar squads. Each rifle squad of 12 men was armed with a .30-caliber BAR in addition to the rifles carried by the rest of the men in the squad. The company weapons platoon was armed with two .30-caliber M1919 light machine guns and three 60mm mortars. The battalion's heavy-weapons company, lettered D, H, and M across the regiment, had eight .30-caliber M1917A1 medium machine guns and six 81mm mortars. The battalion headquarters company included a headquarters section, a communications platoon, an ammunition and pioneer platoon, and an antitank platoon.

It was very rare for a US Army rifle battalion to be at full strength and numbers in the rifle companies might fall below 50 percent. During the Normandy fighting, company-level firepower was enhanced by the addition of .45-caliber Thompson submachine guns and additional BARs. This was subsequently reflected in changes to the table of organization and equipment, adding six BARs and six submachine guns to each rifle company and two submachine guns and six M1919A4 light machine guns to each battalion.

BIBLIOGRAPHY

Ailsby, Christopher (2000). *Hitler's Sky Warriors: German Paratroopers in Action 1939–1945*. Staplehurst: Spellmount.

Anonymous (1945). *Perigamus: A Brief History of the 358th Infantry Regiment 90th Infantry Division*. Oberpfalz: Ferdinand Nickl.

Balkoski, Joseph (2005). *Beyond the Beachhead: The 29th Infantry Division in Normandy*. Kindle Edition.

Blumenson, Martin (1961). *United States Army in World War II, European Theater of Operations: Breakout and Pursuit*. Washington, DC: Center for Military History.

Bradley, Major B. USAF (2005). "Searching for competence: the initial combat experience of untested U.S. Army divisions in World War II – a case study of the 90th Infantry Division, June–July 1944." United States Marine Corps, Command and Staff College.

Brownlee, Romie L. & William J. Mullen III (2015). *Changing an Army: An Oral History of General William E. DePuy, USA Retired*. Charleston, SC: CreateSpace.

Bryan, Lieutenant Colonel Charles B. (1945). *Battle History Third Battalion, 358th Infantry Regiment, 90th Infantry Division*. Prague: Nový Všetisk.

Bull, Stephen (2012). *Second World War Infantry Tactics: The European Theatre*. Barnsley: Pen & Sword.

Calder, Jr., Captain Henry L. (1949). *The Operations of the 2d Battalion, 23d Infantry (2d Infantry Division) in the Attack on Hill 192, West of Berigny, France, 12–16 June 1944 (Normandy Campaign)*. Fort Benning, GA: Staff Department, Infantry School.

Colby, John (1991). *War from the Ground Up: The 90th Division in World War II*. Fort Worth, TX: Eakin Press.

Davies, Brian L. (1974). *German Parachute Forces 1933–45*. New York, NY: Key Uniform Guides.

Department of Military Art and Engineering (1952). *The War in Western Europe, Part 1 (June to December, 1944)*. West Point, NY: US Military Academy.

Department of the Army (1951). *Combat in Russian Forests and Swamps*. CMH 104-2. Washington, DC: Center for Military History.

Dintar, Elmer (1985). *Hero or Coward: Pressures Facing the Soldier in Battle*. London: Frank Cass.

Dittrich, Jim (n.d.). "Col. Glover S. Johns Jr. '931: 'Every Inch A Soldier'." VMI Alumni Association.

Available at https://www.vmialumni.org/colonel-glover-s-johns-jr-31-every-inch-a-soldier/ (accessed February 5, 2025).

Doubler, Michael D. (1988). *Busting the Bocage: American Combined Operations in France 6 June–31 July 1944*. Fort Leavenworth, KS: Combat Studies Institute, Command and General Staff College.

Ewing, Joseph H. (1948). *Twenty Nine, Let's Go! A History of the 29th Infantry Division in World War II*. Washington, DC: Infantry Journal Press.

Feist, U., N. Harms & R. Volstadt (1973). *Fallschirmjäger in Action*. Carrollton, TX: Squadron/Signal Publications.

Graves, Donald E. (2015). *Blood and Steel 2: The Wehrmacht Archive: Retreat to the Reich, September to December 1944*. Barnsley: Pen & Sword. Kindle Edition.

Griesser, Volker (2011). *The Lions of Carentan: Fallschirmjäger Regiment 6, 1943–1945*. Philadelphia, PA: Casemate.

Hahn, F. (2022). *Normandy: From Cotentin to Falaise, June–July 1944*. Philadelphia, PA: Casemate.

Halder, Generaloberst Franz *et al.* (1953). *Analysis of US Field Service Regulations*. FMS P-133. Washington, DC: Office of the Chief of Military History.

Harrison, Gordon A. (1951). *United States Army in World War II, European Theater of Operations: Cross-Channel Attack*. Washington, DC: Center for Military History.

Historical Division, HQ US Army, Europe (1954). *A German Parachute Regiment in Normandy*. FMS B-839. Washington, DC: Combined Arms Research Library.

Holland, James (2019). *Normandy '44*. London: Transworld. Kindle Edition.

Johns, Jr., Glover S. (2002). *The Clay Pigeons of St Lo*. Mechanicsburg, PA: Stackpole.

Kershaw, Alex (2003). *The Bedford Boys: One Small Town's Ultimate D-Day Sacrifice*. London: Simon & Schuster.

Kidd, Captain T. (1946–47). *The Operations of Company M, 116th Infantry (29th Inf. Div.) in the Landing on Omaha Beach, 6–13 June 1944 (Normandy Campaign)*. Fort Benning, GA: The Infantry School.

Lewis, Jon E. (2014). *Voices from D-Day: Eyewitness Accounts of the Battle for Normandy*. London: Robinson.

Lundhigh, Dale (2009). *Show Me the Hero: An Iowa Draftee Joins the 90th Infantry Division during WWII in Europe*. Bloomington, IN: AuthorHouse.

Marshall, S.L.A. (1947). *Men Against Fire: The Problem of Battle Command*. Norman, OK: University of Oklahoma Press.

McKee, Alexander (1984). *Caen: Anvil of Victory*. London: Souvenir Press.

Meindl, Eugen & Richard Schimpf (1946). *3d Parachute Division in Normandy (15 Jan.–16 Jul. 1944)*. ETHINT-78. Washington, DC: Office of the Chief of Military History.

Milano, Vince & Bruce Conner (2001). *Normandiefront: D-Day to Saint-Lo Through German Eyes*. Stroud: The History Press. Kindle Edition.

Mildren, Lieutenant Colonel Frank T. (1947). *The Attack of Hill 192 by the 1st Battalion, 38th Infantry (2nd Division), July 11, 1944. (Normandy Campaign)*. Fort Leavenworth, KS: CMDC CGSC Student Papers.

Moore, Robert E. (1997). *Upstarts: Memories of the 915th Field Artillery Battalion and the 359th Regimental Combat Team of the 90th Division in World War Two*. Unknown: self-published.

Murray, Williamson (1999). "Does Military Culture Matter?" *Orbis* 43.1: 27–42.

Oberkommando des Heeres (1943). Panzer-Nah-Bekämpfung. Lehrfilm Nr. 453. Available at https://youtu.be/ecCUCGQWE04?si=PZFTFVS3oFVRvb4a (accessed February 5, 2025).

Paterson, D. (1995). *Wehrmacht Camouflage Uniforms and Post-War Derivatives*. Europa Militaria 17. Marlborough: Crowood Press.

Quarrie, Bruce (2001). *Fallschirmjäger: German Paratrooper 1935–45*. Warrior 38. Oxford: Osprey.

Roeder, Staff Sergeant George von (1945). *Short History of the 357th Infantry Regiment*. Oberpfalz: Ferdinand Nickl.

Spencer, Henry G. (1984). *Nineteen Days in June 1944*. Kansas City, MO: Lowell Press.

Steckel, Francis C. (1994). "Morale Problems in Combat: American Soldiers in Europe in World War II," *Army History* 31 (Summer 1994): 1–8.

Stuart, Jr., Lieutenant Colonel A.J. (1947). *Infantry Weapons, Observations, and Personal Experiences of the Ordnance Officer, 2d Infantry Division*. Fort Leavenworth, KS: Army Command and General Staff College.

Thomson, H.C. & L. Mayo (1991). *Ordnance Department Procurement and Supply*. Washington, DC: Center for Military History.

Van der Voert, Captain Lee (1947). *The Operations of B Company and of the 1st Battalion, 116th Infantry (29th Infantry Division) on the Elle River and at Couvains North of St. Lo, France, 12–13 June 1944*. Fort Benning, GA: Infantry School.

Villahermosa, Gilberto (2019). *Hitler's Paratroopers in Normandy: The German II Parachute Corps in the Battle for France, 1944*. Barnsley: Pen & Sword Books. Kindle Edition.

War Department (1941). Field Service Regulations, Operations. FM 100-5.

War Department (1942a). *Enemy Air-Borne Forces*. MIS Special Series No. 7. Washington, DC: Military Intelligence Service.

War Department (1942b). *German Tactical Doctrine*. Washington, DC: Military Intelligence Service.

War Department (1943). *The German Squad in Combat*. MIS Special Series No. 9. Washington, DC: Military Intelligence Service.

War Department (1944a). 5th Parachute Div. 6 Jun–24 Jul 1944. Interview with Wilke. FMS B 820.

War Department (1944b). II Parachute Corps, May–6 Jun 1944. Interview with Oberst Ernst Blauensteiner. FMS B-240.

War Department (1944c). Normandy: 3d Parachute Div. to 19 Jul 1944. Interview with Richard Schimpf. FMS B-541.

War Department (1946a). 3d Parachute Division (6 Jun. 1944–8 Mar. 1945). Interview with Richard Schimpf. FMS B-020a.

War Department (1946b). Parachute Regiment 6 in Normandy. Interview with August Freiherr von der Heydte. FMS B-839.

Way, Greg (2019). *Fallschirmjäger! A Collection of Firsthand Accounts and Diaries by German Paratrooper Veterans from the Second World War*. Solihull: Helion.

Weigley, Russell M. (1960). *The American Way of War: A History of United States Military Strategy and Policy*. Bloomington, IN: Indiana University Press.

Zetterling, Nikolai (2000). *Normandy 1944*. Winnipeg: J.J. Fedorowicz.

INDEX